CARLO MARIA MARTINI

BIBLICAL MEDITATIONS

CARLO MARIA MARTINI

THE ACCOUNTS OF THE PASSION

MEDITATIONS

COVENTRY
PRESS

Published in Australia by
Coventry Press
www.coventrypress.com.au
33 Scoresby Road Bayswater VIC 3153
an imprint of Freedom Publishing Books
www.freedompublishingbooks.com.au

ISBN 9780648230373

English translation copyright © Coventry Press 2018

First published in Italy by Editrice Morcelliana 1995

Re-published by
© 2016 Edizioni San Paolo s.r.l,
Piazza Soncino 5 - 20092 Cinisello Balsamo (Milano) - ITALIA
www.edizionisanpaolo.it

Scripture quotations are from the New Revised Standard Version Bible:
Anglicised Catholic Edition, copyright © 1989, 1993, 1995 the Division of
Christian Education of the National Council of the Churches of Christ in the
United States of America.

Catalogue-in-Publication entry is available from the National Library of
Australia http://catalogue.nla.gov.au

Printed in Australia by Brougham Press

THE ACCOUNT
IN MARK'S GOSPEL

THE ACCOUNT
IN LUKE'S GOSPEL

THE ACCOUNT
IN JOHN'S GOSPEL

CONCLUSION

AN INVITATION

The meditations brought together in the current volume take us to the heart of the New Testament message. Cardinal Martini reflects on the account of the Passion in various retreats he based on the canonical gospels. The fact that they have once more been brought together in a single volume allows our reader to access the lively, humble and at the same time, authoritative prose of a preacher who approaches the subject of his preaching in fear and trembling, thus displaying his sincere empathy with all his listeners. It matters little that in this collection there is no obvious connection between all the meditations (in fact the material has been drawn from different contexts): a believer among believers, Martini confesses the consternation which affects anyone preparing to reflect on the mystery of the Passion, clearly highlighting the seriousness, the dramatic nature of this kind of meditation which, when it occurs truthfully, that is, by seeing the consequences for our life, seems rather like a snare that snatches us and sweeps us up.

The approach to the Passion can be very complex and this is why the Archbishop of Milan chooses to view it through a series of biblical 'pictures' drawn from a survey of the four Gospels. The first, in the context of Matthew's account, sees Peter as the protagonist. This is the Peter who is 'each of us,' being 'the man who for the first time is confronted by the inconceivable fact of the Passion, and is affected in the flesh by it because he understands that it is a reflection on himself.' In Peter, the believer recognises the man who, faced with the scandal of Golgotha, sees all his securities disappearing, everything he had thought about himself and Christ. With Peter we learn that 'no one has the true idea of God unless they have known the Crucified one.'

The meditation on the weakness of a God who dies on the cross, a scandal but also our salvation, then suggests to Martini a broader reflection on three possible approaches to meditating on the Passion: one that is historical and emotional, following the sequence of the Stations of the Cross, and marked by compassion. Another of an existential and salvific nature, focused on the 'for me' reference of the Passion and transformed by gratitude. And one that is an expression of Trinitarian contemplation, presented in the language of adoration. The biblical images follow one another in quick succession: Judas, the guards, Pilate. It is an array of faces and events encompassing insults and ignominy to culminate in the most ruinous and incommunicable of silences: 'Only death remains for God; all that remains is for him to allow himself to be killed out of love for those who reject him.'

A 'picture gallery', personalities and encounters, also emerges from his reading of the second Gospel: it is precisely by contemplating the succession of gospel faces which reveal the seed of the kingdom, that it is possible, according to Martini, to meditate on the Passion according to Mark. In Luke, instead, once again with great acumen the Cardinal scrutinises the sketch we find of Peter, and of Mary beneath the cross. The themes of cross, the hour, of exultation and glory, finally, are the ones that fill the pages dedicated to John.

This is a very rich commentary. We have no intention of denying the reader the pleasure of discovering its freshness, both for the richness of its language and for the critical realism that lies behind it; a wise realism, certainly, but because of this, one open to hope.

Looking towards the dawning of the resurrection, the Archbishop of Milan's final word is an announcement that 'concerns everyone, touches individuals, communities, societies. Today there should be no suspicion, sadness, discouragement in us, but a readiness to provide room for that incredible yet true hope that comes from Jesus' resurrection, from the message that God is our Father, that he gives life to all his children, and that no one is excluded from such an extraordinary gift.'

Giuseppe Mazza

THE ACCOUNT
IN MATTHEW'S GOSPEL

1

JESUS' PASSION EDUCATES PETER TO KNOWLEDGE OF HIMSELF AND THE LORD

At that time Jesus said, 'I thank you, Father, Lord of heaven and earth, because you have hidden these things from the wise and the intelligent and have revealed them to infants; yes, Father, for such was your gracious will. All things have been handed over to me by my Father; and no one knows the Son except the Father, and no one knows the Father except the Son and anyone to whom the Son chooses to reveal him.' (Mt 11:25-27).

Lord, we wish to look upon you in order to know the Father. From the cross you reveal the Father to us. Reveal to us, Lord, the mystery of the cross. Help us not to fear it, and allow us to come to know God through it, come to know you, the Son of the Father, come to know ourselves as sinners who are saved.

Give us that spark of understanding of the mystery that you have established in each of us. Make our lives consistent with what you have us understand, and if you want us to experience the doing before the knowing, see that we love before we understand. Give us your Spirit through your death and glorious resurrection.

We adore you, present among us alive, risen, glorious forever. Amen.

Consternation when faced with the mystery of the Passion

I am thinking of an aeroplane that has lumbered down the runway but realises at the last moment that its engines are not powerful enough, nor the strip long enough, for it to take off. This is the way we feel when faced with meditating on the Passion.

It is one thing to look upon the Lord principally to gain an *understanding of ourselves*. It is quite another thing instead to look upon him in order to gain *knowledge of him* (and this cannot be done without entering into the Trinitarian mystery of the Father who gives us the Son, and, above all, without entering into the mystery of the death of God). It is then that we find ourselves completely unprepared.

Hans Urs von Balthasar is one of the few theologians who has tackled the subject of the cross in depth. He compares entering into meditation on the Passion and death of God and what that means for human destiny, with what Isaiah describes in his little foretaste of disaster: an entry into the land of death.

Terror, and the pit, and the snare
are upon you, O inhabitant of the earth!
Whoever flees at the sound of the terror
shall fall into the pit;
and whoever climbs out of the pit
shall be caught in the snare.
For the windows of heaven are opened,
and the foundations of the earth tremble.
The earth is utterly broken,
the earth is torn asunder,
the earth is violently shaken.
The earth staggers like a drunkard
it sways like a hut;
its transgression lies heavy upon it,
and it falls, and will not rise again.
On that day the LORD will punish
the host of heaven in heaven
and on earth the kings of the earth.
They will be gathered together
like prisoners in a pit;
they will be shut up on a prison,
and after many days they will be punished.
Then the moon will be abashed,
and the sun ashamed;
for the LORD of hosts will reign
on Mount Zion and in Jerusalem,
and before his elders he will manifest his glory.

(Is 24:17-23).

According to von Balthasar, these verses evoke all the realities that we are naturally forced to reflect on when we enter the dark mystery of history that is the death of God. In fact, if God dies, everything dies; if the revealing word of God falls silent at a certain point, the whole world falls silent. It is thus that we understand the seriousness, the dramatic nature of this kind of meditation which, when it occurs *truthfully,* that is, by seeing the consequences for our life, seems rather like a snare that snatches us and sweeps us up.

Why the Passion and death of Jesus?

Von Balthasar begins his reflection with a fundamental question, picking up on an expression of Gregory Nazianzen: 'Why was this blood shed?'

Were the Passion and death of the Son of God really necessary after the Incarnation? Theologians are divided on this point. As the Scotists ask, is not the Passion perhaps subordinate to the principal end, the Incarnation, that is the glorification of the Father through his Son, Jesus? Is not the Passion something *accidental*, an adjunct?

If we reject such a theory, since it does not seem to correspond to the data of the tradition, and we place the Passion at the centre instead, as the *end point of God's work,* then another problem arises: sin would become a necessary contribution to God's work because there would be no death of Jesus without sin. If the death of Jesus is the aim, the high point of God's manifestation, then sin becomes essential to this manifestation.

Some theologians resolve the difficulty by identifying two purposes in God's action. Suarez, for example, speaks of a *dual principal reason for the Incarnation.* But this is an attempt to escape the problem: how can a 'dual principal' reason exist? Of its nature, a principal reason is *one.* The attempt, then, only further highlights the difficulty, showing the complexity of the problem, including the theological difficulty for someone who ultimately wants to fully plumb the mystery of the revelation of God's *glory* in the *death* of Christ. The two terms seem to be the antithesis of each other; the revelation of God in the annihilation of God, and this is the mystery of the Passion.

In simple and effective language, von Balthasar states that because God serves, because he washes the feet of his creature, he is revealed in his intimacy. Meditation on the Passion would require an attempt at a *loving entering into* the mystery of a God who washes the feet of human beings and as such, reveals the glorious God, a God who submits himself to human judgement and exploitation, revealing himself as a powerful God.

These are thoughts that the Lord is asking us to explore in greater depth.

Peter face to face with the Passion

Since it is difficult to enter into meditation on the cross, let us permit ourselves to be guided by someone who can help us explore some aspects of the mystery.

I suggest to you that we contemplate how Peter experienced the Passion of Jesus, or how the Passion educates Peter to knowledge of himself and Jesus. It is not yet direct contemplation of the mystery, but it is a way of getting there by degrees, through the difficulties Peter himself experienced. Let us ask him to help us walk his walk, to appreciate his dramatic experience.

By beginning from the words of the gospel we will seek to reconstruct his attitude in prayer. Deep down, *Peter is each one of us,* the man who for the first time is confronted by the inconceivable fact of the Passion and is affected in the flesh by it because he understands that it is a reflection of himself.

We will read from Matthew 14:28 (Peter on the waters) to Matthew 26:75 (Peter finally in tears): from his initial presumption which then turned to fear, of which he was quickly healed, to when he burst into tears revealing how he sees all his securities, everything he had thought about himself and Christ, disappearing.

Presumption and fear

Let us begin with Matthew 14:28.

When he sees Jesus coming toward the boat on the sea, like a ghost, saying: 'Take heart, it is I. Do not be afraid,' Peter replies: 'Lord, if it is you, command me to come to you on the water.'

These are strong words because *walking on the waters* is something that belongs to Yahweh, a characteristic of God in the Old Testament. Peter is quite brazen: asking to do what Jesus is doing and sharing in God's power. Nevertheless, it corresponds to Peter's dream. 'By following Jesus, we have been invested with his power; did he not pass on his powers of expelling demons and healing the sick?' So, we are entering into this *passing on of power* with faith, love, generosity; sharing in God's power. And Jesus assents to this.

> He said, 'Come.' So, Peter got out of the boat, started walking on the water, and came towards Jesus. But when he noticed the strong wind, he became frightened, and beginning to sink, he cried out, 'Lord, save me!' Jesus immediately reached out his hand and caught him, saying to him, 'You of little faith, why did you doubt?' (Mt 14:29-31).

Peter would like to share in Jesus' power but he does not know himself and he does not know that this sharing means *sharing the trials* of Jesus, allowing himself to be overcome by the wind and the waters. He had not considered all this and imagined a simpler game, so when he is overcome he cries out.

His cry reveals the fact that Peter *did not know himself,* was presumptuous, thought that by now he was capable of anything. *Nor did he know Jesus* because at a certain point he no longer trusted him, had not understood that he was the Saviour and that Jesus was there to save him, amidst the force of the strong winds, there where his weakness was manifested.

For Peter, this is *the first experience of the Passion;* an unsuccessful, closed, barely initial experience from which, as also happens in our case, *he does not learn much.* He was probably asking himself what happened and why he allowed himself to be overcome by fright. But the episode remains vague, like many of our experiences that do not come together until a larger one reveals their meaning

Peter's psychological development

Let us now consider all the places that speak of Peter, asking ourselves what they mean for his psychological development.

In Matthew 15:15 ff., Peter says in all simplicity: 'Explain this parable to us,' referring to what Jesus has just said in verse 11, 'it is not what goes into the mouth that defiles a person, but it is what comes out of the mouth that defiles.'

Jesus replies: *'Are you also still without understanding?'*

So, Peter is a man who *has courage,* wants to understand; however, his knowledge of matters concerning God is still embryonic, still on the way, and this shows up throughout his journey.

The following chapter (16:16 ff.) shows us the culminating point of that journey. Peter, speaking for everyone, is the only one who has the courage to speak, and to Jesus' question: *'But who do you say that I am?'* replies: *'You are the Messiah, the Son of the living God.'*

To which Jesus says: 'Blessed are you, Simon son of Jonah! For flesh and blood has not revealed this to you but my Father in heaven. And I tell you, you are Peter, and on this rock I will build my church ... I will give you the keys of the kingdom of heaven ...'

Faced with such promises, Peter felt content: he had responded to the trust the Master placed in him. Jesus had called him from his boat when he was a poor, uncouth fisherman, had trusted him, and he in turn had shown that it had been well placed. It is true that Jesus had said: 'flesh and blood has not revealed this to you' so the revelation is of God: but it was made to him, Peter. God gave him the possibility of giving this testimony to Jesus and, as a consequence, having responsibility in the kingdom.

We can imagine, then, Peter's dismay immediately afterwards: he has barely begun to open his mouth and exercise his functions somewhat, when he is strongly rebuked. In fact, Jesus begins to say openly that he must go to Jerusalem, suffer much at the hands of the elders, chief priests, the scribes, and be killed (the Passion emerges here for the first time). Peter, as a *prudent* man, does not rebuke him in public but takes him aside, thinking to tell the Master honestly something that will be useful to him: '*God forbid it, Lord! This must never happen to you.*'

These words come from the heart, because Peter loves Jesus and believes it is they who should die, since the Master should spare himself for the kingdom. Peter is *very generous* and wishes to die himself, knowing full well that the life they have embarked on meets opposition, gives rise to enmity, difficulties. He is not engaging in self-deception but reasons logically: if the Word falls silent, who will speak? The Word must not be silenced and we must sacrifice ourselves for you.

We can imagine, therefore, his disappointment and dismay at Jesus' response: 'Get behind me, Satan! You are a stumbling block to me; for you are setting your mind not on divine things but on human things.'

Peter had spoken with all the generosity of his heart, had spoken for the good of Jesus and his companions, and here he is, treated like Satan! Confused, he falls silent and fails to do the one thing he should do: ask the Lord to explain himself and show how puzzled he is.

Shortly afterwards he is again fully trusted as the kingdom's 'steward'. He takes centre stage on the Mount of Transfiguration (Mt 17:4) and proclaims: 'Lord, it is good for us to be here.'

Once again, he is speaking on *behalf of everyone,* and has understood that it is up to him to interpret what they are all thinking: '*If you wish, I will make three dwellings here* [or tents], *one for you, one for Moses, and one for Elijah.*'

Seeking to enter into Peter's psychology, I interpret his words as: I will provide! And magnanimously too, because he doesn't mention a tent for himself; however, he is the one who *organises* the kingdom of God. Matthew does not offer a note on this but Luke adds: 'Not knowing what he said.'

Peter's joy explodes on the mountain at having a role and wanting to do whatever was possible to be worthy of the trust placed in him. Given that the kingdom of God is something big, then big things have to be done; hence a dwelling, a tent for each. In the Orient, this is a great luxury. Peter certainly does not reflect much and says whatever comes into his head. He is not even rebuked by Jesus. Then the scene develops, rapidly. A voice comes from on high: 'This is my Son, the Beloved; with him I am well pleased.'

Perhaps Peter could have understood that it is not about setting up tents but about looking upon this Son, seeing how he behaved, how God was revealing him in glory and in poverty; however, all this was not part of Peter's thinking.

When they come down from the mountain and approach the crowd milling around the spot where the disciples had failed to cure the epileptic, Peter, James and John are not devastated by the failed experiment. Peter, with a certain inner satisfaction perhaps, is agreeing with Jesus who says: 'You faithless and perverse generation, how much longer must I be with you? How much longer must I put up with you?' thinking that had it been the three of them, they would have cured him, while the other 'second rate' disciples had failed.

There is also a very interesting episode in the same chapter, full of symbolism (Mt 17:24-27): the one about the temple tax.

Jesus nonchalantly says: 'Cast a hook; take the first fish that comes up; and when you open its mouth you will find a coin.' I am struck by what he says next: 'take that and give it to them for you and me.'

This is a beautiful gesture on Jesus' part, setting aside a coin for himself and Peter, and it almost seems to be a warning: see that we stay together, try to *accommodate yourself to my destiny*, do not pretend to have a different destiny from mine or to look at mine from the outside.

I do not know if Peter had understood the wealth of meaning in this single coin, in Jesus' thoughtfulness. In fact, we see him (included with the other ten) in Matthew 20:24, becoming indignant with the two sons of Zebedee after their mother had approached Jesus asking that the two be seated at his right and left.

Jesus deals with the mother kindly, patiently, without showing irritation, while the disciples, instead, are indignant because they wanted the place for themselves that the mother was asking for her sons. Jesus admonishes them:

> You know that the rulers of the Gentiles lord it over them, and their great ones are tyrants over them. It will not be so among you; but whoever wishes to be great among you must be your servant, and whoever wishes to be first among you must be your slave; just as the Son of Man came not to be served but to serve and to give his life as a ransom for many (20:25-28).

The text does not permit us to know what the apostles were thinking; however, it is clear from what follows that they had still not understood. The Master speaks but they listen without understanding, as happens with us, until an unforeseen and difficult event puts us in touch with reality.

———

We are in a *blind spot*, a psychologically well-described circumstance; there are truths we do not see, about which we are blind or deaf. We hear them spoken, repeated, and we say we have understood them, but we do not assimilate them. Peter is one of these.

Peter's drama

We now come to the final stages of the drama involving Peter, whom we have already seen so ill-prepared (Mt 26:32-35). While Jesus is setting out with the apostles for the Mount of Olives, he exclaims: 'You will all become deserters because of me this night; for it is written, "I will strike the shepherd, and the sheep of the flock will be scattered. "'

This points out something that makes us realise how *weak* the apostles are: you are like sheep. If there is no shepherd you can do nothing. 'But after I am raised up, I will go ahead of you to Galilee.' Peter said to him, 'Though all become deserters because of you, I will never desert you!' Jesus said to him, 'Truly I tell you, this very night, before the cock crows, you will deny me three times!' Peter said to him, 'Even though I must die with you, I will not deny you.' And so said all the disciples.

We have to give Peter credit for his honesty and extraordinary generosity; he really does speak, believing that he fully knows himself, and he says it with all his heart. He has just received the Eucharist, knows that Jesus is in danger and so we cannot think Peter would be speaking lightly. Among other things his words are very beautiful:

———

'Even though I must die with you, I will not deny you.' That *with you* is essential in Christian life.

It could be said that Peter had by now understood the meaning of the single coin for two: I am with you, Lord, in life and in death. How often have we also said that! Peter is saying something very precise and sincere; however, what Jesus had said to them as they went out was 'you will all become deserters' (as the NRSV puts it), but the biblical expression is actually: 'All of you will be made to stumble because of me this night' [as the NKJV puts it. This 'being made to stumble' is the sense of being scandalised]. The scandal is an unforeseen obstacle that works as a trap.

For the disciples it will be the *unforeseen gap* between the idea they had of God and the one that will be revealed during the night. The God of Israel who is great, powerful, vanquishes enemies, the God who will never abandon Jesus, is the idea of God they have learned from the Old Testament. Jesus warns them that they will never know how to resist the gap between what they think and what will take place.

Peter does not accept the warning for himself and believes he finally understands the Lord; he accepts the earlier rebuke, understands that he should always entrust himself to Jesus, then goes to the heart of things or at least tries to go there: 'Even though I must die with you, I will not deny you.'

It is not only presumptuous to think he knows himself, but it is also a mistake. He believes he has the right idea of God but he does not, because no one has the true idea of God unless they have known the Crucified one; yes, he speaks of death, but from what follows it seems he is thinking of an heroic death, the death of a martyr, a glorious death: dying with sword in hand like the Maccabees, like Old Testament heroes; dying while tormenting his enemies about the truth of God and the injustice and shame of those who have attempted to assail his people. Peter has come this far but he does not accept dying in humiliation, silence, the object of public scorn.

We read from the following passage:

> He took with him Peter and the two sons of Zebedee, and began to be grieved and agitated. Then he said to them, 'I am deeply grieved, even to death; remain here and stay awake with me.' And going a little farther, he threw himself on the ground and prayed, 'My Father, if it is possible, let this cup pass from me; yet not what I want but what you want.' Then he came to the disciples and found them sleeping; and he said to Peter, 'So could you not stay awake with me one hour? Stay awake and pray that you may not come into the time of trial; the spirit indeed is willing but the flesh is weak!' (Mt 26:37-56).

It seems impossible that Peter could be so sleepy after such exciting events as those of that evening, after the Eucharist, after the Master's words. Like everyone else, he would have heard that people were running about in the city, plotting, that there were numerous rumours and meetings. None of us gives in to sleep on such occasions; rather are we seized by nervousness and cannot sleep.

Peter's tiredness probably has an element of *psychological disgust* at an unacceptable situation like that of Jesus in the Garden. A little earlier he had said: I will die with you, together we will go to a heroic death, chanting against the enemy. Instead, Jesus is afraid and is making the mistake of revealing himself, showing the truth about himself that others are not prepared to receive.

Thus begins the scandal when faced with a man who is afraid. And from this comes the confusion and desire not to think about it, as happens to all of us with certain suffering of friends, people dear to us, that we do not have the strength to share. It is then that a powerful obliterating force acts on the psyche, the collapse of someone who no longer knows what to do. For Peter to begin to be scandalised and not understand, it was enough for Jesus to reveal his 'true' self and not be so much the Master they relied on, the one who always said the right thing, but a man like others, a friend who needed consoling. 'Their eyes were heavy' the Gospel says: the expression evokes a state of inner blindness, mental confusion weighing on the spirit and making it heavy, opaque, obscured.

Jesus has to pray alone and every time he wakes the disciples he causes *shock*. They see his face, fearful and anguished and doubt begins to surface: Is he truly the Messiah? How can God manifest himself in such a pitiful man? Jesus who humbles himself, looks like filth, staggers about, rocks them to the core, tears down their fortress of mental strength, their idea of how God should manifest himself and should save the one who is faithful to him, who is his Christ.

———

Peter's inner instability finally comes to the point of collapse when 'Judas, one of the twelve, arrived; with him was a large crowd with swords and clubs.' Judas approaches Jesus and kisses him. Jesus does not react but simply says: 'Friend, do what you are here to do.' He is then arrested: 'Then they came and laid hands on Jesus and arrested him. Suddenly, one of those with Jesus put his hand on his sword, drew it and struck the slave of the high priest, cutting off his ear.'

So Peter does make a *final attempt to die as a hero.* Faced with such a crowd of people, his is a desperate but courageous act. The final blow to his miserable sense of security that has once again sought revenge, is Jesus' advice: 'Put your sword back into its place.'

Jesus *publicly rebukes Peter,* who no longer understands anything and asks himself why the Lord called them to follow him if he really wishes to die.

More so because Jesus seems to enter into dialogue with his adversaries: 'Have you come out with swords and clubs to arrest me as though I were a bandit? Day after day I sat in the temple teaching and you did not arrest me. But all this has taken place so that the scriptures of the prophets may be fulfilled.'

If we cannot put our hand to the sword, Peter asks, since these famous legions and angels don't seem to be coming, why is God not saving his anointed one or at least, having him arrested in the temple while the crowd shouts out and a revolt takes place? Instead of at night, like he was a criminal! And he doesn't even react!

Then the text tells us at v. 56: 'Then all the disciples deserted him and fled.'

Their confusion is stressed. It is not total because they would have retained at least their deep-down faith; nevertheless dark thoughts were swirling around in them such that their image of God was in crisis.

Peter is also confused *in his identity:* he no longer knows who he is, what he must do, what his role in the kingdom is. He does not know who this Jesus is who has been abandoned by God. Everything is in turmoil in Peter's mind but he does deeply love his Master so, as it says immediately after v. 58: 'Peter was following him at a distance.'

He does not dare follow up close because by now he no longer knows what to do, but he cannot not follow him.

He is *split as a person.* He had been seized by Christ but at the same time, feels he wants to reject him; following him *at a distance* is the *compromise* that becomes so obvious to everyone in the scene of the triple denial, a public testimony to Peter's bewilderment.

While not knowing *who he is* or *who Jesus is,* Peter provides some answers that paradoxically are true: 'A servant-girl came to him and said, "You also were with Jesus, the Galilean." But he denied it before all of them, saying, "I do not know what you are talking about."'

It is an act of cowardice that did not come from pure fear (Peter was ready to die) but from total bewilderment. To the second question: 'This man was with Jesus of Nazareth,' he denied it: 'I *do not know* the man.'

Matthew appears to be playing with the implied meaning: I really do not know who he is any more. he is an enigma to me too, I can no longer do anything for him since I don't know what he wants and everything is collapsing; God always intervenes on behalf of the just, so this is not a just man. He has fooled us. Peter's state of confusion leads him to swear, and curse the One whom he loves.

The conversion

'At that moment the cock crowed. Then Peter remembered what Jesus had said: "Before the cock crows you will deny me three times." And he went out and wept bitterly.'

The Evangelist is very, very moderate in his language. The crowing of the rooster seems to capture the notion of a man who is still confused, then there is his recall of Jesus' words, hence a gradual perception: 'Jesus truly wanted these things to happen and, if they correspond to his plan, they also correspond to God's plan. So I have understood nothing of God's plan. I have been blind all my life and have lived with a man so long but without understanding him.'

Luke says, 'The Lord turned and looked at Peter' (22:61).

Matthew does not speak of this but we can guess from the scene what Peter is thinking: 'Here is the man I did not understand, whom I always made use of to have a position of privilege and who is now going to die for me.'

A knowledge of Jesus and himself is born. Finally, the veil is torn open and Peter begins to glimpse, amid his tears, that God is revealing himself in Christ who is beaten, insulted. Christ whom he denied and who is going to his death for him. Peter, who had wanted to die for Jesus, now understands: my place is to *let him die for me* since he is better, greater than me. I wanted to do more than him, wanted to go before him. Instead it is he who is going to die for me, worm that I am. All my life I have not succeeded in understanding what he wanted; he offers me his life and I rejected it. This wounding, this shameful *humiliation* allows Peter to begin to understand the mystery of God.

Let us ask him to help us too – through reflection on our own experience – to enter a little into an understanding of the mystery of the Passion and death of the Lord.

'Lord, Son of God crucified, we do not know you so it is difficult to recognise you on your cross, recognise you in our lives!

Open our eyes, show us the meaning of the painful experiences with which you tear open the veil of our ignorance. Allow us to know who the Father is who sent you, who you are; reveal the Father to us in the ignominy of the cross, and who we are who find revelation of you in the humiliation of our poverty.

Lord, that we may follow you with humility through the gift of your Spirit, who lives and reigns with you and the Father, forever and ever. Amen.'

2

THE WEAKNESS OF GOD

'Lord, you once told us: which of you can live with a devouring fire? You see that we are afraid of meditating on your Passion because we are afraid of entering this fire and being consumed by it. We fear that this meditation will move from outer contemplation to inner experience.

Support us in our fear, Lord; obtain for us the grace of knowing your truth and ourselves in it. We ask you to guide us in our poverty and weakness to a knowledge of your poverty and weakness.

You made yourself weak for us; give us the Spirit and be present among us as the Risen One whose kingdom endures forever. Amen.'

There are many ways to meditate on the Passion, many *different approaches* that correspond to the composite nature of human experience in reference to this central, load-bearing point of the whole world's history and experience. Individuals must seek their own. We are called to experience one or other of them, i.e. one or other of these different approaches, at various times in our life.

Three approaches to meditating on the Passion

I would like to consider *three approaches* to meditation on the Passion, that alternate through our lives; some temperaments lean more to one, others to another. None of them, naturally, arrives at the complete mystery, precisely because the Passion is the divine work *par excellence* in which God manifests himself with such power that we can only grasp particular aspects of it.

Above all, we note what the link is between the Passion and the resurrection.

The Passion is not a prelude to the resurrection; it is truly an *end*, the death of Christ and, as such, is definitive in itself. Between Passion and resurrection, then, there is an abyss, and only after having grasped this can we understand how God's power moves from one to the other. Therefore, we need to meditate on the Passion and death of the Son of God in all its *awfulness*, first as it was historically experienced by the people who brought it about in all its *finality.*

Hence, by the Passion we mean the whole, vast mystery that becomes the Paschal Mystery.

Historical and emotional approach

There is a meditative approach that could be called an *emotional, historical* one, that of the Stations of the Cross, for example, based on the gospels or also on traditions, interpretations, added scenes that make Jesus' journey to Calvary more real; it meditates by following Station after

Station, stage by stage of Jesus' suffering, sharing in them emotionally.

This approach is called *historical* because it begins from the description of the Way of the Cross found in the gospels, and it is *emotional* because it supposes our intimate, personal participation chiefly in the sufferings of this man as they appear to us.

Existential and salvific approach

A second approach to reflection that St Paul often insists on, can be called *existential* and *salvific,* where we especially consider the *'for me'* of the Passion: here is the One who gives himself for me and by giving himself, reveals his love, his grace for me and my sinfulness.

It is the consideration of the sinner saved, whose sin and salvation are revealed in the process of the Passion. The Passion is an *extreme case* where human wickedness bursts forth and in the face of which the power of divine salvation is made manifest.

The first approach; the historical and emotional one, suggests *compassion.* The second, the existential and salvific one, suggests *gratitude,* awareness of the truth of one's sinfulness.

The Trinitarian adoration approach

The third approach, that could be called one of *Trinitarian contemplation,* meditates on the Passion by thinking of it as the definitive revelation of God, of the Pascal Mystery. This is the *adoration* approach, contemplation of the truth of God from which also comes, clearly, the truth of humankind caught up in this action.

The truth that is contemplated is that of the powerful God made weak, the God of life who enters death. But it is especially a case of Trinitarian contemplation: the Father who hands over his Son, and the Son handed over, in the twofold meaning of the word '*tradito*' ['betrayed', in the Italian word employed by Martini] – betrayed by human beings and handed over to human beings by the Father.

Certain mystical experiences

Here, mysteries of contemplation and the most mysterious experience of the cross open up because the mystery of *abandonment* appears, Christ handed over, Christ abandoned into the hands of human beings, experiencing abandonment by his Father.

What opens up is the mystical approach of *inner desolation*, all the trials of apparent abandonment by God as experienced by the people who love him, sometimes a long and bitter experience. Whoever endures such painful, purifying, terrible experiences says that no other worldly suffering compares with it. It is the suffering of someone who has placed all his or her hope and love in God and experiences times of darkness, disgust, loneliness, aridity, almost desperation. By reading the works of the mystics we can perceive something of Christ's abandonment that is at the heart of the Passion.

Isaac of Nineveh, for example, speaks of a *mental hell*, a taste of Gehenna where we experience the absence of time: individuals believe they can no longer change something in their lives, can never again find peace. Hope in God and the consolation of faith slip away from the soul and the soul is filled, without pause or respite, with anguish and doubt.

Other than mystics from the Orient, there is a whole Western tradition from St Bernard to Angela of Folino and St Rose of Lima.

The description of this last named saint given by a great historian of the mystics is an interesting one: "Every day the saint was troubled by the most dreadful blurring and darkness of spirit and feeling. She remained hour after hour in such a state of anguish that she did not know if she was on earth or in hell. She stayed there, trembling beneath the unbearable weight of darkness; her will drew her toward love but she felt like a block of ice. Her memory refused to think or at least try to recover an image of earlier consolations; she no longer succeeded in finding them or looking them up. Fear and anguish completely controlled her and her heart cried out: "My God, my God, why have you abandoned me?" But no one replied. The greatest pain was that this evil enveloped her as if it would last forever, as if there were a wall of bronze that made it impossible to exit this labyrinth she was wandering in.'

St Teresa of the Infant Jesus describes something similar, though more delicately put, when she speaks of being in a dark tunnel, moving through it without seeing where it ended. It is the same experience that appears in more painful form in her *Novissima verba*, her last words as recorded by her sister.

St Ignatius, too, went on to Manresa through these trials when, for example, he thought about throwing himself down a well because of the horror of desolation overwhelming him; in more moderate, refined terms but clearly allusive ones, he called them 'terrible experiences.'

In his *Spiritual Exercises* he describes desolation thus: 'I call desolation ... darkness of soul, turmoil of spirit, inclination to what is low and earthly, restlessness rising from many disturbances and temptations that lead to want of faith, want of hope, want of love. The soul is wholly slothful, tepid, sad and separated, as it were, from its Creator and Lord.' (No. 317).

The description is very clear and understands the theology of separation from God, of abandonment by One who does not seem to answer.

It is the abandonment already expressed in so many pages of the Bible, especially in the Books of the Prophets and in the Psalms: only someone who has really possessed the God of the Covenant, only someone who has had, even if only once, the sensation of what it means to possess God in a covenant of love, then knows what feeling abandoned by him means.

However, they are trials not easily put into words and they can even become a very dramatic reality in personal prayer when Jesus asks us to enter into a keener understanding of his Passion.

So what grace should we ask for in meditation? Each should ask for what they feel; no one should make a request beyond their strength. St Francis, at the peak of his mystical experience at La Verna, had asked if he could feel what Christ himself had experienced on the cross, enter into the heart of Christ left derelict and desolate. However, I maintain that it is important, for our journey of faith, to want to understand at least a little of the mystery of the Son of God abandoned by the Father.

A weak God

After having considered the theme of the Passion in general, I am proposing, regarding the *weakness of God*, some pages of the Scriptures for us to reflect on.

1) Matthew 12:18-21 is key to understanding the life of Jesus as well as the Passion. It is a lengthy quotation from the Old Testament by Evangelist Matthew and typical, then, of the Matthean view of Jesus' life.

2) Another meditative path can be found in Matthew 21:33-45: the parable of the vineyard owner told by Jesus in reference to his imminent Passion. It can be interpreted in both existential and salvific terms and Trinitarian terms, going somewhat further than the immediate historical significance of the parable, and seeing it from an experience of Church.

3) Finally, a question: Why the weakness of Christ? Why does he identify with 'the least' (cf. Mt 25)?

There is certainly a link between these two things; and our reading of Chapter 18 of Matthew will guide our reflection.

'He will not wrangle ... nor will anyone hear his voice in the streets.'

We reflect above all on the notion that the Old Testament has of God's power. It presents us (chiefly with the Exodus as background, but already from the moment of creation) with a powerful God who achieves what he wants, to whom nothing is impossible; a God who can wipe out the Egyptian army and devour sinners with fire; a God who shatters the cedars of Lebanon, overturns the depths of the ocean, and makes the mountains tremble like calves leaping in the fields.

The Old Testament teaches us a sense of the irresistible power of Yahweh: 'Who can resist him?' It has us understand that this power and strength are typical of God and he cannot renounce it without renouncing being God, who is power *by his very nature.*

A second consideration which the Old Testament teaches the believer is that God can only but hate evil with all his strength; they are so opposed that they cannot tolerate one another, thus God *destroys evil*, annihilates it. The nature of his power, faced with evil, is that it becomes *anger*, fury. There is no peace between God and evil. The latter must dissolve, feel destroyed by God.

On the basis of these Old Testament truths that we are not asked to reject, Jesus appears as the servant chosen by

God, 'my beloved' (Mt 12:18-21). Matthew has added to Isaiah's text, that simply says 'my chosen.' He has added '*my beloved*' and the notion of the Only Son is already suggested: Jesus, the beloved servant, the chosen one, is not only he who carries out God's works but also, he who brings God close to us, manifests him, is God-with-us. Looking at him we understand who God is.

The *paradox is unexpected* and for the apostles it is very difficult to understand that *this* Jesus could be weak. Already, when the Pharisees met to remove him from their midst, Jesus had departed (v. 15); it was a first sign of weakness.

There is another aspect that had struck Matthew: Jesus was healing everyone but *ordering people not to tell others about it* (v. 16). Jesus was not looking for support, not carrying out a campaign on his own behalf, did not appear to be demonstrating what he was worth. How did this behaviour match his being sent by God? The disciples were wavering.

The prophecy contained in vv. 18-21 ups the ante on this general impression the disciples were gaining: this man is not strong, does not know how to demonstrate his worth and besides, he is obliging us to yield, to pull back along with him. He says he wants to speak to the world but then does not employ the necessary means.

What does the prophecy say? 'I will put my spirit upon him, and he will proclaim justice to the Gentiles. He will not wrangle or cry aloud, nor will anyone hear his voice in the streets' (Is 42:1-2).

For the moment, the disciples' only consolation is that despite their lack of understanding (they will understand only after the resurrection), these are words uttered by the prophet.

We consider how they must have been disturbed by the fact that Jesus was not arguing back. This detail seems to be added by Matthew, who appears to adjust the Hebrew text that says: 'He will not cry or lift up his voice,' while the Gospel says, 'He will not wrangle ...'

But the image of the Messiah who wishes to demonstrate his worth before his enemies is also the image of someone who confronts evil, directly. Why, then, will he not 'wrangle or cry aloud, nor will anyone hear his voice in the streets'?

Why will he not use the means to impress the great masses? On the contrary, 'he will not break a bruised reed or quench a smouldering wick.' So, the Messiah is *meek and mild*, not intrusive but respectful, timid.

Here is the paradox of the strong God who manifests himself as weak, comes to vanquish evil but nevertheless, seems to have such a weak voice that evil can cry out and smother it. Yet the prophecy maintains the character of universal mission, ending in the triumph of justice: 'And in his name the Gentiles will hope' (v. 21)

So, God is revealed to him, and not only is God content with him but the world too, deep down, awaits him.

The prophecy in Matthew can already be interpreted in terms of the Passion and death of Jesus: 'He will not break a bruised reed,' but he himself will be broken on account of such weakness; nor will he 'quench a smouldering wick,' but others would snuff it because he did not know how to demonstrate his worth.

A question wells up from the heart: you, great God, who rule the heavens and govern the earth and have everything to hand, why do you expose yourself to the ongoing scandal of the good, the so-called just, throughout all of history?

God does not annihilate, does not destroy. He allows himself to be mocked by the challenge of someone who says: 'If there is a God, let him come down and wipe me out.' We are faced with a mysterious paradox whereby we live in this world where the unjust triumph and those who take no notice of God flourish.

We ourselves, then, experience the mystery of God's weakness; these realities are part of our everyday experience.

The vineyard owner

Matthew 21:33-45 recounts the parable Jesus delivered in Jerusalem at a time when he is locked in tense battle with his adversaries.

The 'vineyard' is the people of Israel whom God loves and for whom God had done so much. God, the owner, 'leased it to tenants and went to another country.'

It is the owner's mistake; if he thought so much of the vineyard he should have stayed there, should have looked after it himself, not entrusted it to others.

It is the story of God's weakness, entrusting things he loves most dearly to human beings. He entrusts his vineyard, his people, to others in whom he should place no trust but whom, in real terms, he does trust, and that looks silly to us. He is deluding himself.

God's weakness lies in the fact that *he trusts human freedom*.

Yet such faith, as we were saying, is poorly placed: 'when the harvest time had come, he sent his slaves to the tenants to collect his produce. But the tenants seized his slaves and beat one, killed another, and stoned another.' They were thinking: 'The vineyard is ours so we can do what we want with it.' Since the landowner had left them free, they gained confidence and forgot that the freedom was given them so they would cultivate the vineyard and see that it bore fruit.

Faced with the first servants coming to demand the produce, the tenants behave like children in front of a new teacher; beginning with some pranks to see how she reacts, to see if she can keep discipline or not, and if they see that all is going well, they carry on, getting worse as they go along. In fact, the tenants cautiously welcome the slaves to the table, pretend to get upset, then someone beats one of them, another grabs a second … they are testing the owner's strength: perhaps he is not very capable, perhaps he won't punish us, perhaps the vineyard is ours. 'Again, he sent other slaves, more than the first, and they treated them in the same way.'

There are more servants, however, and the scene is repeated. The tenants think the owner does not know how to show his mettle, that he is too weak.

And then the ultimate test: 'Finally he sent his son to them, saying, "They will respect my son."'

———

By now the tenants have become so evil that they are no longer able to appreciate the situation. They ask themselves: 'How come he is sending us his son, after the earlier slaves have been belted up so much? Does it mean he doesn't care about his son, maybe he wants to get rid of him; but he is naïve, deluded, and really does not have the power we were afraid of.' They said to themselves, 'This is the heir; come, let us kill him and get his inheritance.' So, they seized him, threw him out of the vineyard, and killed him.'

Let us try to re-read the parable from the owner's point of view.

He wants to put his trust in them: 'I am giving this vineyard which I am very fond of to these people, to give them the opportunity to get on in life and render an important service to themselves as well.' Then, when he sends his slaves and sees how worse for wear they are for it, he thinks: 'Perhaps it was a difficult time, so I need to help them understand and if they are reasonable people, they will be convinced.'

In the end he sends his son, risks everything for the trust he has in his tenants: 'At least they will respect my son and finally understand what they are doing.'

The owner's weakness, then, is *love,* the willingness to promote the people's freedom by doing good, risking everything. The cross manifests this saving love at any cost, the *incredible trust* God has in each of us.

It seems strange that the owner sends his son, believing he may be killed. Yet Scripture says that God hands over his Son – without reservation – to human beings, because he needs to trust them to the ultimate degree.

———

That the owner is not weak is shown by the words that follow, showing God's fury. Jesus says: 'Now when the owner of the vineyard comes, what will he do with those tenants?' [that is, when the period of trial and freedom is over]. The parable's listeners reply:

> 'He will put those wretches to a miserable death, and lease the vineyard to other tenants who will give him the produce at the harvest time.' Jesus said to them, 'Have you never read in the scriptures: "The stone that the builders rejected has become the corner stone; this was the Lord's doing and it is amazing in our eyes?" The one who falls on this stone will be broken to pieces; and it will crush anyone on whom it falls' (Mt 21:41-43).

The cross is not only God's power, it is also *terrible judgement* and can be so, precisely because it is the test where God holds nothing back from our freedom, and wants to give us the opportunity to express our freedom in service. In giving us this freedom, however, he also gives us the opposite possibility. God's weakness is not a mere rhetorical device (I am strong, but to humiliate you who believe in strength, I make myself weak); instead, God enters a relationship of dialogue with human freedom, going to a limit that for us is inconceivable. The words of the Sermon on the Mount are incredible to us – the absence of defence to the point of yielding to our enemy. Yet, the Father hands over his Son in the hope that the enemy will understand.

'... you did it to me.'

We now consider the weakness of God who becomes incarnate in the little ones and the weak, in the Church, the community, in history. Let us reflect on Chapter 18 of Matthew, his discourse on the Church, the first goal of which is the little ones: 'Who is the greatest in the kingdom of heaven?' He called a child, whom he put among them, and said, 'Truly I tell you, unless you change and become like children, you will never enter the kingdom of heaven ... whoever welcomes one such child in my name welcomes me ... if any of you put a stumbling block before one of these little ones ... Take care that you do not despise one of these little ones ...' (cf. vv. 1-11).

He then continues, 'What do you think? If a shepherd has a hundred sheep, and one of them has gone astray, does he not leave the ninety-nine on the mountains and go in search of the one that went astray? So, it is not the will of your Father in heaven that one of these little ones should be lost.'

From here he moves on to kindness to a fellow sinner: 'If another member of the Church sins against you, go and point out the fault when the two of you are alone ... But if you are not listened to, take one or two others along with you ...'

He finally gives the command to pardon unreservedly, *'seventy-seven times'* (cf. vv. 12-22).

A contemporary biblical scholar, commenting on this chapter of Matthew's, after developing his thoughts on the individual person in the Christian community, offers a line from René Guisan: 'The only individualism the Gospel authorises is that of the lost sheep.'

The Book of Matthew, then, is an ecclesial Gospel in which the meaning of the individual, the unique person, appears.

If we carefully reread Chapter 18 in this light, we note that within this discourse on the Church, one of its most characteristic motifs is in fact the weight given to the *individual*, especially in the first part focused on the reality of the little ones, i.e. lowly, vacillating believers not considered as a group, state or class, but in their individuality.

The number 'one' recurs five times: 'whoever welcomes *one* such child,' 'If any of you put a stumb-ling block before *one* of these little ones,' 'Take care that you do not despise *one* of these little ones,' 'If a shepherd has a hundred sheep and *one* of them has gone astray,' 'So it is not the will of your Father in heaven that *one* of these little ones should be lost.'

In Matthew 25:40 we read: 'Truly I tell you, just as you did it to one of the least of these who are members of my family, you did it to me.'

We are clearly in the context of God's judgement on people's deeds.

According to the commentary by the biblical scholar I have already mentioned, the whole community is called on by the Lord to adopt precise attitudes toward individual believers who find themselves on the periphery, who are without social influence. The community owes these people acceptance, solicitous attention, consideration, and shares responsibility for these individuals' possible ruin.

In the apocryphal Gospel of Thomas it says that the lost sheep was the fattest in the flock, but Matthew 18:12 speaks of any sheep, so long as it is lost. That is enough for the flock to go looking for it. Just one lonely, disoriented sheep unable to find a way to get back with the others: no other reason is needed for having to go looking for it without hesitation. And beyond the parable? A member of the community is lost and he or she is a lowly, weak believer who is struggling on the journey of faith. That person's individuality is enough to mobilise the Church to go looking for the person.

The reason for so much concern and love for the individual is very simple: everyone counts for much in the Father's eyes. The Father does not resign himself to standing by passively while someone is lost. We are entering into the *logic of the Father* then: it is the little ones he has so much at heart, the waverers, the marginalised, the lost.

Linking back to our reflection again, God seeks out the weak, and *this is why* he makes himself weak. Whoever recognises the Son of God in this weakness begins to understand God's plans, to understand something of his paradoxical ways of revealing himself.

Jesus says that we have done to him what we have done to a brother or sister, not just out of a comfortable or even merciful accommodation, but because this way, we enter into the mystery of God who reveals himself in weakness and so we can perceive something of God's life.

So, there is a *double way*: recognition of God in the little one and the weak; recognition, in weakness, of Christ, God's strength.

'I thank you, Lord, because you manifest yourself to us in unexpected ways, in ever new and surprising ways. We pray that not a fragment of this manifestation is overlooked but is immediately applied to all the situations in which we recognise that someone near us represents you, reveals your face.

Grant, Lord, that we may live a practical life illumined and deepened by the knowledge and love of your Passion and death. Guide us in this difficult search in which we can easily deceive ourselves. See that the words we say and hear are perceived as serious words that one day could be our condemnation if they remain just words.

Save us, Lord, through your mercy, you who give us your Spirit and live and reign forever and ever. Amen.'

3

THE VULNERABILITY OF GOD

'Virgin Mary, Mother of the Lord, you followed your Son laboriously up the Mount of the Passion. Grant that we may toil and walk along this road to be with your Son and to understand that he is the gift of the Father and the Spirit. Amen.'

So, let us continue on our journey even though, while climbing the Mount of the Passion, we feel all the pain of it.

We are proposing to meditate on Jesus and Judas, Jesus and the guards, Jesus and Pilate. Faced with each episode we will identify with Jesus, Judas, the guards, Pilate, asking ourselves what happened and why. Everything should be experienced by *immersing ourselves* in the scene, seeking to grasp its message for today.

Judas: meanness and illusions of grandeur

The reference is to certain passages in Matthew: 26:14-16, 20, 26, 47-50; 27:3-10.

Who is Judas? There is no gospel figure that has so stirred the imagination of novelists and film-makers; a figure who attracts psychologists and scholars, first because he represents so many of the contradictions of human existence. We will not try to provide an umpteenth new reconstruction of his prior history and motives, but by looking at things very simply, on the basis of the quoted passages, we will attempt a response.

Judas is a man who combines meanness and illusions of grandeur – his *meanness* manifests itself in reference to money; it seems such an unimportant thing in such a tragic scene to be thinking of financial gain, but if one is mean, then the banality of it emerges in even the most dramatic situations. Judas also has *illusions of grandeur*: his death is 'grand' in some ways; he seeks to be a self-centred tragedy taking place in front of everyone.

He is probably disappointed with Jesus. We cannot believe that Jesus had chosen so badly right at the outset that he did not know the man had no interest in him. As an apostle, Judas was probably yearning for something, was enthusiastic and committed, but after some time, *disappointed in God*; because God was manifesting himself this way, because he did not intervene; why was this Master going from weakness to weakness? It was unacceptable. God was not with him!

He was disappointed at how God was manifesting himself in Jesus and *how Jesus was manifesting the power of Yahweh*, which Judas was possibly hoping for as the political and moral rebirth of the nation.

Jesus was not the *leader* he was expecting and, if he was not that, it was so much more worth pursuing his own dream of grandeur and being opposed to him. Judas is thinking of something big, but he does not move away like a mediocre person would. He just leaves disappointed, and that is it! He is resentful and upset: If Jesus is doing something bad for the people, then I will hinder him and, if he must fall, it is better he fall quickly.

Disappointed in himself, he allows himself to be seduced by a mirage of revenge, resentment that suddenly overwhelms him. In fact, he says, 'I have sinned by betraying innocent blood' (Mt 27:4). It means he had grasped the truth but had allowed himself to be overcome by political emotion, personal resentment, bitterness as well as his own meanness.

How does Jesus behave where Judas is concerned? In one contemplation we admire God's *vulnerability* in Jesus. He behaves as one would with a free, loyal, honest person, that is, by admonishing, speaking clearly, trying to shake him up. However, he does not stop him but offers himself to Judas, leaves him be. We need to add: Jesus facilitates Judas' task. We are at the limits of paradox.

In this regard there are *two passages* that make us think. One, the clearer one, is John 13:27, 'Do quickly what you are going to do.' This way he gives Judas permission to cut loose. It was almost as if Jesus was saying, in the language of freedom: do what you think is right, follow right through on what you think is your view of God and things, act freely and see what comes of it.

Another, more mysterious passage is in Matthew: Jesus' response to Judas' kiss (26:49-50). It is already significant that on the way to the Mount of Olives, in a place Judas knew, he allows himself to be taken; had he fled to Galilee, things would have panned out differently. We have the impression that Jesus gave up, handed himself over, and he responds to Judas' kiss with a mysterious sentence: 'Friend, do what you are here to do.' (The Greek text says, 'Friend, this is what you are here for'). It is not a case of real encouragement, but he limits himself to checking him: 'Look at who you are, look at what you are doing! If you want, carry this out, but be careful what image of yourself is being offered by what you are doing.'

We ask ourselves, in following this account, what comes from the fact that Judas is ultimately trying to exercise his freedom, his resentment and his anxiety to fulfil some grand plan, disappointed with what Jesus is not.

What comes from it is Judas' *desperation*; seeing how his dream is disintegrating and how an innocent man is condemned, he recognises that everything has gone amiss. Reading the account, we need to keep in mind what is found in Chapter 27 of Matthew, where it tells of Jesus' trial and death. He also dies for Judas (again we observe the God-human relationship: God grants people the freedom to act against themselves, in Christ, and offers himself for this mistaken freedom). It will be Judas' fault if he does not understand (as Peter, instead, will understand) that God was for him.

Who, then is Judas? Who is the traitor? Who is this man thrown into confusion, who abuses his freedom to the point of seeing that it had all gone away? *It is me*, it is each of us. It is me, disappointed, bitter, who has a false image of God and myself and lets the mistaken presumptions of my disappointment emerge, rather than reflecting on things. In order not to admit it, I attach myself to some mirage of revenge, spite, and end up wherever.

Who is Jesus in my eyes? He is *every brother or sister of mine* who is a victim of my spitefulness, revenge, the false use of my freedom. This dramatic game between Jesus and Judas, this substantial misunderstanding of a man who does not want to look at himself and runs up against others continues in, around and right beside us.

God no longer sends us his Son directly (we recall the parable of the murderous vineyard tenants); he sends us our brothers and sisters, *he entrusts us to one another.* We are able to do what we want with each brother or sister of ours, we can make the worst use of our freedom. It is terrifying to think that the use of human freedom in regard to others has no limits, that God entrusts each brother and sister to us, and us to others.

The judgement scene looks like this: 'Have you recognised yourselves? What use have you made of your mutual freedom? Did you welcome me? Were you welcomed? Or did you make use of the other as Judas did with Jesus, as an object of revenge, getting even, as an outlet for your disillusioned thirst to be someone?'

We need to reason clearly, not only at the *familial* level, but also the *social and political* level: group revenge, spitefulness, personal motives all come into play in all the conflict that goes on in national and international, social and political life. They constitute the forces that incite people to act against others, that spur some on to vaunt their pride, perhaps masked behind humanitarian ends but always at the expense of others. Jesus' appeal is to the nations, every social group, every class: 'What use have you made of your strength, your power, the fact that other individuals and groups have been entrusted to you?'

The guards: frustration and revenge

The second consideration focuses on Jesus and the guards: Matthew 26:65-68. 'Then the high priest tore his clothes and said: "He has blasphemed." Then they spat in his face and struck him ...'

It is not clear who carries this out; it would seem to be the Sanhedrin, but just the same, it helps to think rather that it is a reference to the soldiers, the servants of the Sanhedrin, when they see that Jesus has lost his dignity, and they vent themselves on him: Luke 22:63-65 seems to indicate this with greater clarity.

Let us enter into this account and ask ourselves who are the men who are slapping, beating, mocking: 'Prophesy to us, you Messiah! Who is it that struck you?' (Some translations have 'Christ' in place of Messiah, the only time the Gospels use the term.) Jesus is ridiculed at the core of his mission and the Father is ridiculed in Jesus, in the most precious gift he makes to human beings. Their choice is a truly wretched one.

So, *who are these men*? They are most unhappy individuals, poorly paid people whose lives are miserable, at the mercy of whomever commands them, sends them hither or thither; people without dignity whose family, if they have one, is full of woe. People who lie awake at night without knowing why. People who detest the service they give, accustomed as they are to being ill-treated by whomever is in power, so, *in need of revenge*. Every now and again, when these men have power, they exercise it. Perhaps they have often been beaten or unjustly punished, and now here is someone they can take advantage of, show that they are someone, they have dignity.

They are the *human nature in each of us*, alternating between obsequious servility and revenge on whomever seems lesser, lower than us. Revenge takes so many devious forms: for example, there is a cultural revenge (those who know how to say things versus those who don't), another to do with one's upbringing (those with refined manners versus those without). Revenge can be everything that serves to keep us in a state of superiority. These men, then, take their frustrations out on Jesus – their hours of oppressive guard duty, their grey existence without future, always with the risk that something will happen to them.

What does Jesus do? According to the Gospel passage, Jesus does and says nothing; being the Son of God given to us, he lets things happen.

We would like to ask in prayer to enter into the heart of the crucified and humiliated Lord:

'Lord, what were you experiencing during that moment you felt abandoned by everyone, while outside the apostles were denying you and nobody came to testify on your behalf? By now you were nothing for nobody.'

John (18:23) records Jesus' words to the men striking him. They help us to understand the significance of his attitude: 'But if I have spoken rightly, why do you strike me?'

God's appeal to human freedom, once again, is powerful: look at yourselves and at what is happening to you. Why are you doing this? What series of frustrations, what times of servility, what fears have forced you to such a point?

Jesus is the *vulnerability of God, who offers himself to human beings* as a mirror of their pettiness, in the desire that they can see themselves, be horrified by themselves and accept the salvation that this humiliated Jesus offers them in his silence.

It is his vulnerability that God offers me in every weak brother or sister of mine who does not know how to react, who perhaps simply does not have the presence of mind to respond to a barbed comment of mine, a bitter word. God offers himself to us in Jesus to heal us, and offers himself to us in our brothers and sisters to confound us and at the same time free us, get us to see who we are.

Pilate: human respect (Mt 27:11-16)

Who is Pilate? He is a bureaucrat attached to his office; the most important thing for him is not to lose his position.

However, he is caught between two tensions as often happens: by orders from on high, schemes, political storms, things that have to be done; and from below by worries and the malcontented. On a daily basis, Pilate experienced all the bitter effort of maintaining a *certain balance* between these two tensions, of not losing his career and not displeasing anyone – not his conscience and certainly not the emperor, or the people, because while basically the emperor was far away, he had to live with the people.

We are faced with the drama of a poor man who is cultured, has a sense of dignity, basic honesty, even if he has serious faults. He also appears to be a man who has a line to hold but wants to salvage everything: his post, the emperor's good graces, good relationships with the Jewish authorities, and the people's favour. Being a cunning man, he looks for ways out: when he gets the idea of Barabbas he believes he can get by and keep everyone satisfied. The people will be happy because he is releasing a prisoner; the emperor will be happy because he won't be receiving complaints; and his conscience is at ease because Barabbas deserved the death penalty. But the compromise does not come off and Pilate even becomes naïve when he presents himself before an irate mob thinking he can succeed in convincing them. That shows the level of bewilderment he had reached and where his political savvy had ended up: he is no longer in touch with the normal reactions of the people.

He desperately tries to extricate himself from the situation, like a lion in a cage, hoping for a way out that does not go against his conscience, something whereby he can save himself and the man who has done nothing wrong. Life had probably not prepared him for a situation like this, where something ordinary had suddenly become difficult and humiliating. He looks for all kinds of solutions but not the only just one, that is, to make use of his freedom and dignity.

What does Jesus do? He says the only thing he can possibly say at that moment: 'You say so.'

Here too, as with Judas and the guards, there is a reference to the *dignity of the person*: 'You see, you know. If I am guilty I am ready to be condemned. If I am not, ask your conscience a question; if you are a free man, then show yourself to be such, let your dignity triumph.'

I like to imagine that Pilate had had a moment of uncertainty and had asked himself: 'Am I an official or am I a man? If I am a man, I have my freedom and this person interests me; perhaps he has something to tell me, perhaps he can explain to me why I feel so ill at ease, what is happening to me; if we sit down together he will tell me something about himself.'

And what would Jesus have said to him? More or less what was contained in his 'You say so': 'You have the power to condemn me and you are free to do so if you recognise that I am guilty. And also, if you find no fault in me I am still in your hands. However, ask yourself: What unease is gnawing at you? What are you afraid of? What do you want?' For the first time in his life, Pilate would have felt he was in a *man to man* exchange with an individual who would not flatter him but nor would he reject him. He would speak freely with him. I imagine that had he made this gesture he would have felt free of human respect toward the emperor and the Sanhedrin, and able to face the risk of a people's revolt.

The conversation with Jesus could make a man *genuine*, free from so many absurd fears for which all of a sudden, he feels ridiculous. Jesus also gives his life for Pilate, to reveal a way out for him. This is the *liberating engagement* Jesus would like to have with each of us. The only solution for Pilate was to come down to the level of his brother and speak to him, because the *person* was more important than laws, career, bureaucracy.

Jesus teaches us that in any situation, there is always the possibility of a sincere relationship with him, a relationship that can lead us back to our genuine self. He teaches us that we can always find a moment of fear, even in the most intricate situations, the most absurd and ridiculous ones, in which to discover their profound meaning, understand our true relationship with people and give back importance to the human being rather than to things and structures.

We are before Jesus who reveals God's vulnerability to us, who allows himself to be dealt with as we please, because he wants each of us to recognise him. We are Pilate with a façade, honour, a label to be saved at all cost.

Let us ask ourselves what there is of Pilate in us, what prevents us from being free, what our fears are, our labels, the masks and clothing we wear in public and that stop us from taking risks. Let us try to discover all our absurdities, our ability to neglect and trample on the other for appearances sake, to maintain the façade, or the important post, or the good opinion of the people regarding our honour, reputation, the respect we are owed.

Speak with me – the Lord tells us – make yourself free, know that at any moment you can be driven to trample on the other in order to defend a world you have constructed, to put yourself in an irreparable situation, without any way out.

By entrusting himself to us, by his vulnerability, God reveals to us his willingness to enlighten us on who we are and what we can be if we recognise him in his truth.

'Lord, you have manifested your Son to us in the poverty of a man. Reveal to us what we are.

May the blood of your wounds not be in vain for us, and may we be healed through your wounds; by virtue of this blood may each of us rediscover the freedom we are destined for. Amen.'

4

THE DEATH OF GOD

We have considered how Jesus offers his friendship
to Judas, the guards, Pilate; a friendship that could have
given them a way out of their wickedness, spitefulness,
resentment, the fear they were all locked into. Just the same,
none of them allows themselves to be won over by this
offer, and not because they were particularly bad; they were
simply human beings, *people like us.*

Human beings do not accept the offer of friendship God
makes in Jesus when they see that it brings with it a truth
about themselves and, as a consequence, the need to exit the
circle that holds them in its grip.

The incommunicability of death

Only death remains for God; it only remains for God to
allow himself to be killed out of love for those who reject
him.

Every death bears the sign of an absolute *mystery* and
the experience of an absolute *incommunicability.* We can
understand almost nothing of what happens to a dying
person, and at the end we find a total inability to give and
receive.

———

But if it is impossible for us to understand a person's death, then how can we understand Jesus' death and the mystery that surrounds it; a *finality* in death as it is for any individual, and one from which only God can emerge? Jesus allows himself to be swallowed up by the depths, an unrepeatable, incommunicable experience, *experience of non-experience.*

In this regard, certain mysterious words from the Book of Revelation come to mind: 'When the Lamb opened the seventh seal there was silence in heaven for about half an hour' (8:1).

This 'half an hour' points precisely to the inability to understand, being struck dumb by everything.

On the other hand, Job's three friends (who had set out 'to go and console and comfort him') did not recognise him when they saw him from a distance; they raised their voices and wept aloud and sat with him on the ground seven days and seven nights without saying a word (cf. Job 2:11).

To approach the mysteries of suffering and death means to be overwhelmed and be unable to say anything.

Following Matthew, we will now meditate on the insults Jesus receives while on the cross, on his final moments and lastly, on some of the events immediately following his death.

The insults heaped on Jesus

A characteristic of crucifixion, regarded as a most shameful punishment, was to make a man die while exposing him to insult and public shame. The very position of the condemned individual pointed to ridicule.

Bystanders

The bystanders, passers-by, were people Jesus may or may not have known, people who had heard him speak and maybe sometimes had listened to his teaching. Though they might have thought he spoke well, they had then gone on their way and now, finding him on the cross, were wondering at the way he had finished up. Naturally, the taste for evil forever found in each of us began to emerge: if God were truly in him he would not have died like this. It means he had deceived us and the hours spent listening to him were a waste of time. In fact, the Gospel notes that they were 'shaking their heads.'

There is a semblance of reason in these people; when just people are persecuted and at the end of their strength, right thinking people say: 'If things have ended up badly there has to be something behind it.' Some might have recalled something Jesus said: 'He said the temple would be destroyed (a statement that would certainly have been passed on by word of mouth since it was so striking), let him save himself, show us his power!' Others would have listened to Jesus speaking at length, and remembering that he even claimed to be the Son of God, were saying: 'If he is God's beloved Son, let him come down from the cross!'

Such reasoning, that seems to be common sense, implies *a certain notion of God*: God is great, powerful, victorious;

whoever trusts in him, even though tested by dark moments, will triumph in the end. If he doesn't triumph it means God is not with him.'

From this idea of God comes the insult that becomes a *blasphemy* (as the Greek text calls it), an insult that is a kind of revenge: 'This man believed he was telling us whatever, but his words sounded really odd to us. Now, finally, we can see that we simple folk were right.' It is the response of those who were not overly committed, had not wanted to understand.

Again, *before Jesus,* even in death, *people reveal themselves,* shows up the miserliness, mediocrity of their thinking, expressed so spontaneously that people believe they are saying the most sensible things.

The theologians

Then there are the *theologians,* those who felt most threatened in their image of God and by Jesus' way of acting: the high priests, scribes, elders, or in other words, the categories who held cultural and religious power and, to some extent, administrative power. They were all reasonable, serious people who were laughing at and mocking Jesus because the fraud had been unmasked: 'For a while this man impressed us and we had taken him somewhat seriously. But now we see he was worth nothing and cannot save himself.'

It is interesting to see how the mindset of the theologians and learned is revealed: 'He saved others,' (they acknowledged Jesus' miraculous activity, which impressed them) 'but he cannot save himself.' So, in that saving of others there was something not quite right. 'When we cried out that he was expelling demons in the name of Beelzebub, he got angry, but in reality, we were right. Our *theological reasoning*, with which we unmasked his position (the people were beginning to dislike him), is revealed to be correct because he cannot save himself, while we do grant that he did save others. If he is the king of Israel as he said, as he seemed to be saying at the last session of the Sanhedrin and in front of Pilate, let him come down from the cross and we will believe him.'

The religious element comes into play: 'Come down from the cross, show you have the power to save yourself and then we will believe you can also save Israel.' A quotation from the Bible is added to the theological reasoning: 'For he said, "I am God's Son."' (cf. Ws 2:18-20).

'If he is truly bound up with the Father, let God confirm the truth of this bond.'

The thieves

The third category of individual is the thieves crucified with Jesus. The people on the street insult him because they felt cheated and tricked by him. The priests, representatives of culture, did so because he threatened them by his teachings; the two thieves insult him (as it seems by comparison with Luke's account, or simply by reconsidering the situation) because he does not help them: 'Seeing that right now you are a wretch like us, decide you can show that you are "someone", and save us!'

We think of Jesus suffering and in agony listening to these words that touch the *very core of his mission*; salvation, his being the Son of God and King of Israel, the new Temple, the ability to save others, his trust in his Father. All Jesus' prerogatives are put to the test and tied to a very subtle thread: 'If you come down from the cross we will believe; but if you stay there we cannot accept anything of what you said you came for.'

Us

Let us reflect on *what we would have said to Jesus* as people on the street, even without arriving at insult. Let us place ourselves in the category of those who, deep down, did not see clarity in what was happening. Perhaps we too would have said: 'We believe in you, but come down, if you would just make the slightest gesture, right now many would believe in you! You have worked so many miracles. If you came in order to be accepted, what would it cost you to work another miracle to be acclaimed? Make everyone fall to their knees and cry: "he was truly the Son of God, we are mistaken!"'

Instead, Jesus calls directly on the Father's aid with the inspired and infallible words of Psalm 22.

I suggest each of us asks the Crucified One, in contemplation. 'Why?' The Lord will reply: 'Reflect on the notion of God bound up with the request of the priests, scribes, thieves, the people: the notion of a powerful, victorious God saving by an act of power. But the image of God I bear on behalf of the Father is one of a God who takes on your weakness, vulnerability and submits himself fully to human freedom. How could I come down from the cross without denying all this? What triumph would the image of a powerful God be? And I would not be bringing my mission to completion because, at the decisive moment, I would be denying the vulnerability of God placed into human hands. I would have given credit to your freedom, but only up to a certain point. That way it would be thought that God had not been serious in his offer of friendship. He did not submit himself to all the consequences, so deep down he does not love human beings or their freedom.' How could we claim that God's mercy is without limits if at a certain point he were to say: 'Enough, the experiment is over, it has gone too far, don't you understand?'

So let us ask ourselves, then: *'Which God do we believe in?'* Is he truly the God of the Gospel, the God of the revelation by Jesus Christ, the God whom no philosopher has been able to think up or imagine, who reveals himself in the Crucified One, whom we cannot recognise except through a *total* conversion of the heart?

Let us ask the Lord and his Mother, who experienced this dramatic and serious revelation of the Father and impressed it on our hearts, to help us understand how pagan we still are in our concept of God: we want a God who tests us but who also saves us before things end up badly. A God who does not have the total trust in us that he had in Jesus.

Spontaneously and paganly, without wanting it, we always return to an image of God who is *at our service*, at the service of our power, our success, not a God in whom we can and must trust totally, just as Jesus trusted him.

For us, God is an ocean into which we want to throw ourselves, but with a small lifebuoy because this way, if the sea does not sustain us, we will succeed in saving ourselves.

Jesus faces us with our paganism and asks us: 'Are you ready to open your heart to the God of the Gospel and everything such acceptance implies?'

The final moments

'From noon on, darkness came over the whole land until three in the afternoon.' This succinct and weighty sentence seems to recall the darkness that filled the abyss at the beginning of creation. Hans von Balthasar, in one of his studies, offers a very strict approach to its interpretation. He wants to provide all the realism possible to the *dereliction* of Christ. By exploring some of the theories expounded especially by Luther and Calvin, he proposes reading into this mysterious moment of the Lord's life the verification of that state of abandonment that is felt in embryonic, rudimentary form by the Christian mystics in spiritual desolation. Jesus would have felt this state of abandonment to its maximum degree, the *suffering of the damned*, of *hell*. He would have come to understand the very extreme of human desperation, not as *sinfulness* and rebellion against God but as *anguish* and suffering.

However, it is certain that Jesus dies as head of the Mystical Body. So, all the experiences we have and that we can objectify and communicate to others only with difficulty, what we sense as abandonment, anguish, loneliness, lack of faith, hope and love of God; all this focus is a *real way to come to knowledge of Christ.*

Each of us, beginning with our own experience, is invited to grasp in Jesus' final words the point of reference for perceiving what is going on in us. Thus even in abandonment, Jesus shows that he is a friend and reveals to us who we are, and through which hidden mysteries (the *tunnel* that St Teresa of the Infant Jesus speaks of) we can achieve knowledge of God and freedom of heart.

One current of Western mysticism has often thought that the experience of aridity, tedium, effort, obscurity, the night, cannot be eliminated in the spiritual person; they are simply *paths leading upwards* from the heaviness of the flesh, through purification, toward contemplation of God's light.

In truth, we need to interpret this *Christologically,* in the light of the Gospel: we are called to be where Christ is, to know God as Christ has given us to know him. And since Christ's power is revealed in weakness, God's light is revealed in the darkness of the hours on the cross. God's glory and hope are manifested in Jesus' cry of pain and abandonment. Thus, we too, in some way, are called through ways suggested to us by Jesus to a *different* understanding of God than we have.

———

The question returns: Why does God make himself known through the cross? Could not Jesus come down from it and save us in an easier way? Would he, then, have really taken seriously the abyss of the world's and human wickedness? Again we are urged to seek to understand his paradoxical way of dying.

Jesus' death is not glorious, not extraordinary. By the grace of God there are some enlightened deaths, deaths of people in whom we can breathe in something of the serenity, the peace of God. This is the power of the Risen One poured into our most tragic experience, and sometimes it transforms it. But Jesus' death was not like that.

Misunderstanding follows his last words: they think he is calling on Elijah and offer him a sponge soaked in vinegar. There is confusion but no spectacle of grandeur, no people at prayer, admiring. Everything develops between the serious and the ridiculous, amid people who are accustomed to seeing the condemned die. Jesus cries out again in a loud voice, a cry without words, full of mystery.

Jesus' death is dramatic. It does not have the aura of serenity or peace: he falls into the abyss of human wickedness that swallows him.

We note that while John and Luke present us with the transfigured aspect of Jesus' death, Matthew and Mark show us a more dramatic and bitter side. This latter (it should not let us forget the former) represents his sharing in so many deaths without grandeur, that are really the deaths of the majority of men and women of this earth.

In a story told by Ivo Andric about the Franciscans in Bosnia (they had to be typical of the times, people living under Turkish domination, constantly in situations of difficulty and suffering), we read that one of them, a zealous, rustic character, is called by a farmer to attend a dying man. He is accompanied up the mountains where there is a Christian bandit in a cave, someone who has fought against the Turks all his life, has killed people and now refuses to see a priest when he is dying. It becomes a giant struggle: the simple friar, full of enthusiasm, has tough words to say about hell, the crucified Lord. The other man turns his head to the wall and does not respond. At a certain point the man turns back and the friar understands that he is on the verge of expiring; he gives him absolution and is aware that the other has accepted it in some way. He leaves content, thinking: 'I have saved a man.' Later, the farmer comes back and calls him again. He runs toward the mountains again and sees the man crucified on a tree at the edge of a ravine, below the cave. The friar asks: 'Why, Lord, why does he die like this? I had given him absolution, could he not die more calmly? Why, Lord, have you done this to me?'

The story suggests very well how we would like the final moments of our life to pan out: in calm, serenity, resignation, but also how these moments could be strange, mysterious, unforeseeable. Jesus' death shares in the unforeseeable nature of the human experience of death.

We can only but adore the mystery of the Lord who has associated himself with each of us. We do not know what our experience will be but we know that the Lord, through love, has prepared the way for us and will meet us there.

After death

After Jesus gave up his spirit, the veil of the temple was torn in two, the earth shook, rocks split and the tombs of the dead opened, then bodies were seen moving about, the centurion was terrified. In general, exegetes remain perplexed by the Evangelist's description. To me, however, it seems that the description seeks to express the inexpressible.

It is true, that faced with Christ's death there is only silence; but silence with human and cosmic resonance that can be grasped in faith.

We will limit ourselves to considering what happens to the centurion and the guards. 'Now when the centurion and those with him, who were keeping watch over Jesus, saw the earthquake and what took place, they were terrified and said, "Truly this man was God's Son!"' (Mt 27:54).

Here we have the *first proclamation about Jesus* and the first revelation of the effects of the paradox of God in human experience. At the least suitable moment, humanly speaking, when all the bitterness of Jesus' death is evident, and the people are hurrying about with indifference, the centurion and guards who are from outside cannot find language to describe the events and exclaim: 'Despite everything, this Jesus was someone, perhaps the Son of God!'

How did they arrive at this intuition? Here is where the paradox of God is manifested, revealed in a manner most contrary to what we would have expected. What the passers-by, people on the street, the priests had not understood, the soldiers had. We could surmise that there would be some among them who had earlier insulted Jesus and who were then standing very close to him, who were beginning to understand God's patience, his way of being and acting.

Whoever was looking on at a distance had not grasped the meaning of the scene, while those who had seen Jesus up close had not failed to gain the impression that God was in the Crucified One, even if everyone else said the opposite. The centurion and guards were prepared, then, and when the external signs impinged on their imagination with their strong sense of divinity, the step was completed: 'Truly Jesus was someone, truly he was loved by God.'

Let us ask the Lord that we may not reflect on him only from a distance (Who are you? Why have you acted like this? Was it really necessary? Why must we also do the same?), but come close to him like the soldiers did, despite themselves, so that all our mental searching dissolves in contact with the truth.

If we have the courage to exit the circle of people who cry out from a distance without understanding, and speak to him, enter into the mystery of his heart, then for us too there will be a new revelation and *the veil of the temple will be torn asunder*, the veil that is our *old understanding of God*, a great and powerful God who vanquishes the enemy,

81

crushes his adversary. The mysterious God covered by a veil preserving his intangibility, absolute otherness, inaccessibility, is now made weak, poor, vulnerable in Jesus and can enter into the heart of every human being to become an *experience* of life.

It is an experience both of Christ and human suffering that we are afraid of, that we look on from a distance, from which we defend ourselves with conventional words and that we will finally have the courage to approach, despite it apparently being bitter, incomprehensible, absurd.

'Lord, through the intercession of Mary, your Mother, grant that we may stand with the soldiers beneath the cross and have on our lips the words with which the Church asks us to remain close to the Crucified One:
Holy Mother! pierce me through,
in my heart each wound renew,
of my Savior crucified.
Amen.'

THE ACCOUNT
IN MARK'S GOSPEL

1

THE MYSTERY OF THE
SON OF MAN

Introduction

To better understand the account of the Passion in Mark's
Gospel, I will commence with a meditation entitled: *the
mystery of the Son of Man*, that includes passages given us by
Mark between Chapter 8 and Chapter 10.

We are entering the hidden depths of the kingdom of
God. As a consequence, our understanding of what we
will now be reading must occur more in prayer than in any
theoretical consideration of what we are listening to.

Somehow, we must now more deeply understand what
St Paul sought to comprehend when he says in the *Letter to
the Philippians*: 'I want to know Christ and the power of his
resurrection and the sharing of his sufferings' (Phil 3:10).

Already in the earlier chapters of Mark we can guess that
the fate of the seed that has been trampled on and smothered
is, in the final analysis, the fate of Jesus himself. The seed is
the word we read about in Chapter 4: the evangelical word,
but the evangelical word is Jesus.

The kingdom presented obscurely in the parables as a hidden mystery, growth that takes place in obscurity, a laborious and difficult growth, is revealed more clearly in the second part of Mark as the mystery of the Son of Man.

The catechumen, the one being instructed who said 'yes' to Jesus the Son of God, *beside the lake* when he heard the call, experiences an introduction to a new and unexpected situation through the trials of faith he is led through in following Christ. It is a situation in which the laws of personal encounter, humility, expectation, patience are in force. This is the school that Jesus runs in the first eight chapters of Mark.

Being with him leads the disciples gradually to understand how the life they have embraced is not one where the laws of efficiency, success, power are in place, but the laws of hiddenness, personal encounter, smallness.

After Chapter 8 this veiled understanding of the mystery, that occurs only through hints, becomes clearer. The second part of Mark's Gospel begins.

We need to preface this by saying that Mark's Gospel is clearly divided into two more or less equal parts that differ between them in several respects. For example, there are words that occur frequently in the first part and no longer in the second, and vice versa. Words characteristic of the first part are verbs like: understand, inability to understand, see, having hardness of heart; listen, know, hide, reveal; verbs that indicate how Jesus is asking for understanding of the kingdom through trust in his word. He complains that people have closed hearts, that the disciples do not understand. Jesus wants to arouse their attention in such a way that their minds will be drawn to what he is about to manifest.

At a certain point, however, Jesus' requests changes: the insistence is no longer on understanding, on opening their eyes, but on doing something for the kingdom, giving themselves, their lives, paying in person. Here, then, are the ideas typical of the second part: only the one who loses his life will save it; the need to leave house, brother and sister, parents, children for the gospel; also hand, foot and eye are to be sacrificed for the kingdom.

In the first part it is about *understanding* the kingdom. In the second part it is a case of *entering* the kingdom.

Which event is it that marks the passage from attention to the kingdom to entering it? Which event leads from the first to the second phase of Jesus' teaching?

It is the episode of Peter's messianic confession at Caesarea Philippi, a central point after which we find a change in the themes of Jesus' preaching. And it is in the second part that he dedicates himself, in particular, to a more careful formation of the group of Twelve. In the first part they follow him, see what he does; in the second he turns to them more frequently, more intimately.

Why does Peter's confession have such a central role? Because this is the moment when the kingdom on earth begins. The fact that Jesus is recognised in his true identity by this tiny group, as a small mustard seed by comparison with the then world, just Peter and the other eleven, marks the beginning of the kingdom Jesus comes to bring on earth.

This fact alters the whole content of Jesus' preaching. He begins to speak no longer in riddles but clearly.

So let us look at certain elements of the second part of Mark's Gospel in particular, the predictions of the Passion: the first of which immediately follows Peter's confession while the other two follow at regular intervals, one per chapter. This rhythmic succession in Mark is clearly intentional.

First prediction of the Passion: Mark 8:31-37

'Then he began to teach them.' Evidently it is a new beginning, a new way of speaking, a new moment in the formation of the Twelve.

What is Jesus teaching? That the son of Man must undergo great suffering, and be rejected by the elders, the chief priests and the scribes, and be killed, and after three days rise again. He said all this quite openly.

Jesus is teaching one thing that was never mentioned earlier and that penetrates right to the heart of his mystery. He teaches that 'he must', that is, that what he is starting out on belongs to the plan of salvation, to God's plan for the redemption of humankind. 'The Son of Man': this is a mysterious label. In the apocalyptic tradition it has a glorious connotation of Messiah, but here it is employed in a context of extreme humility and total humiliation. 'Must undergo great suffering and be rejected': be rejected by priests, the high priests, scribes, that is, by the people of culture, the social categories that then counted as something. 'And be killed and after three days rise again. He said all this quite openly.' This gives us to understand that up till now, Jesus has not spoken openly. He has attracted his followers – especially the Twelve – with the charm exuding from his personality, miraculous power and kindness. He has filled them with trust in him. Now that they are a small, compact group he can address them clearly.

And the clear words are extremely hard ones because he is speaking of death: being rejected and killed. It is true that death appears within the perspective of resurrection, but in such mysterious form that the disciples still do not understand.

The mystery therefore is present in its entirety and immediately creates a sense of consternation and bewilderment in the Twelve expressed immediately afterwards in Peter's intervention (vv. 32b-33). It shows the reaction of the common individual, each of us: 'This mustn't be, can't happen, makes no sense.' It expresses our inability to understand the mystery of God as he shows himself to us in his reality and truth, in Jesus Christ.

When we pass from an outward appreciation of the mystery of God in Christ to the true understanding, that is, to the mystery of Christ rejected who died for us, our first reaction could well be expressed in Peter's words: 'How come? Why? This absolutely cannot be ...'

Probably the Twelve can well understand that if this were to happen to the Master, something similar would be destined for them. Their future fate will certainly not be comfortable. The horizon is becoming cloudy and murky.

Then Jesus tells Peter that he understands nothing of God's plan. In Peter the Twelve are confronted with God's true plan, faced with the tough reality of the Lord's project, a most mysterious reality that is unacceptable from the point of view of common human logic. However, because of the affection they have for Jesus, because they are with him, they can no longer reject him. They have contrary inward reactions but are completely captured by the Lord's personality, so much so that he knows he can speak openly to them. Nevertheless, his words are very tough.

Then in vv. 34-37 the focus shifts to the disciples. Jesus has spoken of himself. He has spoken clearly of his destiny and that gives rise to amazement, consternation, bewilderment in the apostles. Now he gradually begins to shift his direction, his own mystery as the Son of Man, to the life and direction of those who are following him.

Thus, his words: 'If any want to become my followers, let them deny themselves' (v. 34).

If we think about Peter who denies Jesus by saying he does not know him, we can say that 'denying oneself' is trying to say: I do not know myself, I no longer take my life into account, I no longer consider myself. This is how Paul would speak – summing up his life – in his address to the elders at Ephesus as recorded in Acts 20:18-24.

Jesus goes on: '... take up your cross,' meaning all the inconveniences that following Christ brings with it, and: 'follow me.'

The force of this whole sentence lies in the verb 'follow me'. The other things said before and after are the necessary preliminaries for being able to be with Jesus and to continue being with him.

We can broaden our consideration of everything specified in the following Chapters, especially Chapter 10, regarding this following of Christ. Here we have only the first of the indications as to what the mystery of the kingdom implies. The same requirement is specified in various forms in the Chapters that follow.

I have brought together some passages to show that in practice, Jesus' teaching to the small group of the Twelve can be summed up thus: 'Whoever has accepted the personal call to follow me must accept me as I am' (cf. Mk 10:43-45, 29, 38, 13:13).

How is Jesus' identity and activity described? He explains that where and how he is, the others must be too. For example, he says he came: 'not to be served but to serve; whoever wants to be like me, then, must be everyone's servant.'

'I have left everything: the Son of Man has nowhere to lay his head; hence, I can ask you to leave father, mother, fields, children and everything.'

'I came to you as someone owning nothing; hence, I can ask you to leave the wealth that does not fit in with the kingdom of heaven.'

'I will first drink the chalice of the Passion; hence, I can ask you to drink my chalice.'

'I accept contradiction, being rejected by the majority of my people; you too must accept contradictions, opposition, from wherever it comes because the Son of Man was rejected first.'

In other words, Jesus, in the texts we have been drawing on, asks us to courageously choose a life similar to his, to choose it in our heart, because encountering one or other external situation does not depend on us; instead, what depends on us is choosing in our heart a life as close as possible to his way of living among human beings.

It will not always depend on us to choose the humblest service, the least glamorous position, the simplest outward circumstance, but it will depend on us to have the desire in our heart to be where he is, as far as possible.

So, between positions of greater or lesser prestige and power, choose the lesser. Between circumstance of greater or lesser wealth, choose the latter. Between positions of comfortable or inconvenient service, choose the inconvenient.

This is how the training for evangelical choices takes place in the second part of Mark. Jesus places himself before them, presents himself, and invites each one to be where he is, at least with the heart, by desire, because this is the way to come to a deeper understanding of the gospel.

It is about an extremely important choice because, beyond all the theologies and theories, it involves the capacity to understand the gospel from within.

When the fundamental choice is not made of being where Jesus is, not only in the outward activity described in the first part of Mark, but along the path that leads to the cross as we find it in the second, then it will not be possible to identify the other gospel truths, give them their rightful place, understand the relationship between individual realities and their background that can ensure that everything is in its right place.

Every true conversion, every true appreciation of the Spirit, every ability to understand the situations in which we find ourselves – our situation in the world, the current situation of the Church – begins with renewed adherence to the life of Jesus as it is presented to us in the second part of Mark.

It is the evangelical secret that gives us the way to understand our place, the Church's place in the world; it is at the heart of Jesus' demands.

Second prediction of the Passion: Mark 9:31-32

The second prediction is very short: 'For he was teaching his disciples, saying to them: "The Son of Man is to be betrayed into human hands, and they will kill him, and three days after being killed he will rise again." But they did not understand what he was saying and were afraid to ask him.'

Here we have Jesus, even closer to his disciples, forming them to the one essential point and presenting the one central mystery of the gospel: himself, his death and resurrection.

Nevertheless, Mark has us note how difficult this mystery is and how it needs to be continuously rethought, in new situations, amid the new demands of our spiritual life and its growth.

Jesus' proposal is absolutely incomprehensible, it cannot be compared with any other human proposal.

In fact, no human proposal would dare speak of death and resurrection: we are at the heart of the complete and pure faith demanded of the disciples, as the only way to arrive at a true grasp of what evangelical life signifies.

Third prediction of the Passion: Mark 10:32-34

The final prediction is broader than those preceding it: 'They were on the road, going up to Jerusalem, and Jesus was walking ahead of them; they were amazed, and those who followed were afraid ...'

Mark seems to want to give us courage by saying that the apostles took some time to understand. Jesus was loved by them, stayed among them and even went ahead of them, and they could only but follow him. They felt intense attraction to him, but as for really understanding the heart of the mystery, there was still a long way to go. And the road was an extremely exhausting one.

> He took the Twelve aside again and began to tell them what was to happen to him, saying, 'See, we are going up to Jerusalem, and the Son of Man will be handed over to the chief priests and the scribes and they will condemn him to death; then they will mock him and spit upon him, and flog him, and kill him; and after three days he will rise again.'

Here is the mystery once more, with a notable insistence on the moments where Jesus is rejected and despised. This becomes a new request to the apostles to trust in him and to accept all of the mystery in its totality, because there is no resurrection without passing through suffering.

What could the catechumen conclude who was gradually being educated through this lesson in understanding the central mystery of the kingdom of God?

The catechumen was implicitly invited – and that goes for us too – to adore the mystery of the divine plan, in prayer first of all, recognising that it is extremely difficult to comprehend. Every time we run up against it, not only in our imagination but in reality, we experience an instinctive inability to adapt ourselves, and the need to persist with a prayer that we can accept the Christ just as he is.

Secondly, the catechumen is encouraged, along with us, to thank the Lord for showing himself so clearly and without any desire to deceive us. This is so we can praise him when we experience his death and resurrection in ourselves, so that we will then certainly be at the heart of the gospel.

All the situations that at first sight seem to be incomprehensible and unacceptable – when the cry rises in us: 'Anything, but not this!' – are in reality situations that place us at the centre of the manifestation of the mystery of God.

Finally, the catechumen is asked, and so are we, to pray insistently, asking Jesus to hold us close to him and take us into the heart of things with him, convinced that such acceptance is the key to discernment, to analysing the different mindsets operating in us and the Church.

We pray that at this point the mentalities and behaviours that are not gospel-based will disperse and dissolve. All the

---

dreams, castles in the air, all the purely human projects –
may they diminish and only the truth of the gospel remain.
The catechumen is educated gradually and insistently to be
aware that this is the fundamental revelation of the Son of
Man. It is the mystery that, if we are to enter into it, requires
us to overcome purely human planning and locate ourselves
at the heart of the kingdom of God.

2

THE PASSION OF JESUS

In the three predictions, Jesus announces the way of the Passion and then courageously takes it to the end.

We are invited to follow him, at least emotionally, in contemplation, coming closer to him with our heart so we can somehow realise what Peter could not, even though he wanted to – the 'I must die with you' (Mk 14:31).

We understand how Peter would have wanted to be with the Master to the end, but he would do so later, after having passed through the tough lesson Jesus was preparing to give him by undergoing the Passion.

Questions on the Passion

For various reasons, reflection on the Passion is always very difficult and it was already so for the early Church.

It was especially difficult to respond to the questions of how historically such things could happen. It implies an inexplicable series of errors, hasty and clumsy decisions, chain reactions, hand-balling of responsibility between one or other of the main players. In fact, there was no reason for Jesus to be put to death!

The way in which this was so quickly arrived at, in a confusion of passions, mistakes, prevarications, and fears certainly embarrasses whoever tries to recount it.

Mark goes into great detail to gradually explain the range of tragic and dramatic events that in themselves were not adequately motivated.

Another difficult question presented itself to the early Church and the catechumen meditating on the Passion: how could a death be great?

All those people who, for various reasons, have some familiarity with the mystery of death, know how all the rhetoric immediately ceases when we are faced with it.

There is nothing less human than death. Usually a dying person looks awkward or perhaps tormented, incredulous. There is no situation where human beings are less themselves than at the moment of death.

As something it is difficult to provide a meaning for, death is nonsensical for the person experiencing it. The dead person represents something incomprehensible, something that should not be.

Now, considering that such a reality that is nonsense for life, was faced by the Lord Jesus, it makes it the mystery of mysteries. Why Jesus, life itself, should have wanted to reduce himself to all the expressions of human degradation that are part of death, is truly without explanation.

The early Church feels this mystery profoundly because the real figure of the crucified Jesus lay before it. The big problem was how to interpret this, since of itself it seemed impossible to do so. How do we give it meaning? And this from two points of view:

1) From a human point of view: how do we interpret the rest of life's realities that seem to lack meaning, seem to be pure loss, lack, and therefore unwanted?

2) From God's point of view: how could God be with Jesus even in the Passion and death? Did he not perhaps abandon him?

The response

These are the problems that disturbed the heart of the early Christians who were meditating on the Passion. The lengthy account in each of the Gospels is the response to such questions.

It takes up two chapters in Mark; he gives it quite disproportionate space compared to the rest. For the catechumen and for each of us, it means that the Passion demands lengthy consideration. We need to give much contemplation to the Lord's Passion and let it be a large part of our understanding of him. The account introduces a difficult mystery, and in turn is presented through some facts that give it meaning.

The fundamental meaning is given by Isaiah: *Quia ipse voluit*. Because it was his own will (Is 53:7 in the Vulgate but see the Hebrew text, Is 53:10a, 12c).

The Passion is not accidental, but it is Jesus himself who ultimately accepted the extreme humiliation. It then begins to acquire meaning because it becomes a human act by Jesus. What episodes emphasise this *Quia ipse voluit*?

The anointing at Bethany where Jesus says: 'She has done what she could; she has anointed my body beforehand for its burial' (Mk 14:8). Jesus goes toward the mystery of human degradation and consciously accepts it.

During the Last Supper: 'So the Son of Man goes as it is written of him' (14:21). Jesus, then, is entering a plan that is the Father's plan. Again, during the Supper and even more clearly: 'This is my body of the covenant which is poured out for many' (14:24). The Eucharist shows that Jesus anticipates and fully accepts the Passion.

And finally, at Gethsemane, the last words to take up this theme once more: 'Yet, not what I want but what you want' (14:36).

The entire Passion is meditated upon by returning it, so to speak, to the intimacy of the Lord's heart; he went to meet this tragic fate voluntarily.

In this regard I would like to emphasise an aspect that follows from the manner in which the Passion is presented by Mark: Jesus went to meet death because he wanted to help us to the farthest limit; he did not want to pull back from any of the consequences of *being with us*, entrusting himself to us completely. He fulfilled the mission of being with his own by accepting the ultimate dramatic consequences of entrusting himself to human beings with good will and the desire to help them.

From our reflections on the *Quia ipse voluit* we can conclude that the only thing capable of giving meaning to our sufferings is for us, too, to arrive at accepting them with him.

Sometimes this is easy enough for suffering we manage to perceive as such (for example, illnesses that are not too serious), and that we can take from God's hands patiently, offering it up for others. However, when suffering becomes part of us, when it becomes a difficulty identified with our very being, when we end up finding ourselves in situations where it is extremely difficult to recognise any sense in them, then acceptance becomes ever more problematic because we do not feel free nor detached in the face of them. We can struggle for years in a state of unease, possibly unconscious intolerance and inward rebellion against circumstances we are unable to accept. At times, indeed, the hardest thing to accept is precisely ourselves.

Jesus teaches us that until we come to a conscious and free acceptance, our sufferings have no real meaning; we begin to discover this when, in some way, we have stared them in the face like he did, and have accepted them with him.

I believe this is the key to understanding the *why* of Jesus' Passion: *Quia ipse voluit.*

A picture gallery

Coming to the Passion itself, I suggest a way of meditating on it that fits in with the structure of Mark. In his Gospel, the Passion is a whole series of little pictures following on from one another, pictures that describe human situations, people bumping up against one another.

It is not so much a chain of events that is reported, nor is it a study of the chain of causes, even though this is present.

Mark's way of telling us the story is rather by presenting a series of pictures in which different personalities enter into direct comparison with Jesus, each experiencing the mystery of their own call and stance before the kingdom.

In the Passion, Jesus continues his mission of proclaiming the mystery of the kingdom to the most diverse and distant kinds of people, to those who seem to reject him, in order to *be with us* to the end.

In some ways, even the parable of the sower is verified: Jesus presents himself as the seed in different soils and meets a different fate in each of them.

It is possible, then, to meditate on the Passion as a series of episodes, situations in which Jesus heroically continues to be the Good Teacher who teaches us to lose our life in order to gain it, to deny ourselves, to take up our cross, to make ourselves the servant and slave of everyone, in short, to carry out the plan spelt out in Chapters 9 and 10 of Mark.

I suggest you contemplate the pictures one by one, considering the mystery of the kingdom as the evangelical seed that receives different responses. I am indicating 14 of them so they can possibly serve as Stations of the Cross:

1. *Jesus and Judas*
2. *Jesus and the guards*
3. *Jesus and the Sanhedrin*
4. *Jesus and Peter*
5. *Jesus and Pilate*
6. *Jesus and Barabbas with the crowd*
7. *Jesus and the soldiers*
8. *Jesus and Simon of Cyrene*

———

9. *Jesus and the men crucified with him*
10. *Jesus and his mockers*
11. *Jesus and the Father*
12. *Jesus and the centurion*
13. *Jesus and the women around the cross*
14. *Jesus and his friends*

It is a gallery of people who are compared with the seed of the kingdom. Each has a different response before Jesus, who adopts the same attitude of availability and the offer of salvation to each.

There is a certain orderly development in these scenes, an ongoing crescendo of humiliation as far as the tenth scene, the mockers.

Another important detail in these scenes is Jesus' silence. He speaks briefly at the beginning, speaks to Judas, the guards, the High Priest, and to Pilate in the fourth scene. And then he falls silent. They all revolve around Jesus like a dramatic merry-go-round and he dominates them all with his silence. We contemplate the contrast between the individuals getting upset or doing or saying one thing or another and Jesus, in his silent presence at the centre, dominating a chaotic and confused situation.

By just existing, by just *being there*, Jesus speaks, Jesus judges.

Then come Jesus' last words as he cries out: 'My God, my God, why have you forsaken me?' (15:34), that express both the zenith and the nadir of the journey of the cross, even to the extreme of desolation, but also manifest immense trust (Ps 22 {21}:1, 20-23).

———

At the centre of it all, in the eleventh scene, is Jesus' cry, his invocation of the Father. From this point a gradual flow of consolation and peace begins. Already in the Passion, as it has been recounted, a sense of consolation and peace are born that will last until the sepulchre, preparing the way for the resurrection.

We can note this progression and then the gradual entry of a new atmosphere when Jesus is on the cross. We savour the change that the crucified Lord mysteriously brings about in those nearby: the women, the friends.

The scenes of the Passion for which I have offered you some starting points, should become a frequent topic for our contemplation because they are the daily antidote to the worldly atmosphere we live in and that Paul speaks of when writing to the *Ephesians:*

> Finally, be strong in the Lord and in the strength of his power. Put on the whole armour of God, so that you may be able to stand against the wiles of the devil. For our struggle is not against enemies of blood and flesh, but against the rulers, against the authorities, against the cosmic powers of this present darkness, against the spiritual forces of evil in the heavenly places. Therefore, take up the whole armour of God, so that you may be able to withstand on that evil day, and having done everything, to stand firm. Stand, therefore, and fasten the belt of truth around your waist, and put on the breastplate of righteousness. As shoes for your

feet put on whatever will make you ready to proclaim the gospel of peace. With all of these, take the shield of faith with which you will be able to quench all the flaming arrows of the evil one. Take the helmet of salvation, and the sword of the spirit, which is the word of God' (6:10-17).

In the careful contemplation of the Passion, the knots of the hard-to-fathom questions are undone and judgements on ambiguous situations are clarified. Compared with this paradigm, all the excess falls off and that which remains instead is evangelically valid.

Perhaps it is because of the lack of reflection, meditation, contemplation on Jesus' Passion that we witness so much confusion today. The Passion plays a predominant part in the gospels, precisely to offer us a secure element of discernment.

THE ACCOUNT
IN LUKE'S GOSPEL

1

JESUS BETWEEN SUCCESS AND INCOMPREHENSION

'Lord Jesus, you went to the Passion out of love for us. Let each of us allow ourselves to be attracted by you so that we may follow you wherever you lead us.'

Introduction

We are not capable of understanding Jesus' Passion; it only speaks to us through God's grace. In meditating on it, then, each one will react according to the grace corresponding to his or her prayerful state. It could be a state of purification, one of seeking, or one of enlightenment. Indeed, we cannot force a response in ourselves different from our current state.

I sum up my reflection in the following terms: Jesus gives himself to us as the ever good evangelical word that yearns to bear fruit. The word is also defenceless. We receive it starting from our reckoning and suspicions, hence the possibility of our rejecting it. Jesus allows himself to be rejected.

———

We will make reference to three predictions of the Passion found in Luke (9:18-23, 43-45; 18:32-34).

Jesus is still in public life, still moving between acceptance and incomprehension, this latter highlighted above all by those who were called to understand him better. That was their calling and mission. Hence, Jesus is living between 'success and incomprehension.' We will see that our life too takes place between success and incomprehension. Already the location of the three predictions makes us see that significantly they are placed differently by comparison with Mark's Gospel where they appear at regular intervals (Mk 8:31; 9:31; 10:32) from Chapter 8 to Chapter 10, in preparation for the entry into Jerusalem in Chapter 11; there, they are part of the narrative rhythm.

In Luke, instead, two are very close to one another in Chapter 9 and the other found in Chapter 18, so they almost frame the entire journey of Jesus to Jerusalem, along with miracles and instructions (especially about abandonment to the Father, detachment from wealth, other people ...) that in some ways constitute the warp and weft of the journey.

We ask ourselves in prayer what the circumstance is in which these predictions are made; how Jesus conducts himself; how the disciples respond and, finally, how we become involved.

'But who do you say that I am?': Luke 9:18-22

Looking at it as part of a broader setting, the first prediction is placed within the context of Peter's confession.

Jesus is praying alone – again Luke introduces him with the favourite scene of Jesus at prayer – when the disciples approach him and he asks them: 'Who do the crowds say that I am?' We are amazed that Jesus wants to know what the people think of him: clearly it is a rhetorical question aimed at eliciting what the disciples are inwardly thinking. Just the same, he begins with the broader question. It is not that he is insensitive to what the people are saying about him (we will need to bear this in mind when Jesus speaks of the humiliations to be heaped on him), because he wants a response to his message. He is not preaching to be mocked but to be listened to, so he wants to know what his word is producing and even what people think of him. In short, he recognises that being accepted is a fundamental part of his perspective, so it is important to know whether people see him as a magician or an odd-bod.

The response itself is rather comforting – John the Baptist, Elijah, an ancient prophet arisen – because it picks up on certain characteristics of Jesus:

John the Baptist: the people see him as an austere person, living a simple life. Besides, John the Baptist had fearlessly spoken out against Herod. So, the people respect Jesus as a courageous man capable of speaking the truth to everyone.

Elijah is the powerful prophet, one of the greatest of the prophetic figures who spoke in God's name, resisted the powerful and the kings of his time; the people think Jesus speaks in God's name, that he does great works.

A prophet; that is, God's spokesperson; the crowd are right, they understand that God's action is present in Jesus not as some little known prophet but as the greatest.

111

Naturally, Jesus is convinced that this is not enough, so he then asks the apostles: 'But who do you say that I am?'

The question is a bold one and points to a clear relationship. We often try to avoid questions of the kind because the answers could disappoint us and we prefer to maintain the opinion others have of us or that we would like them to have.

Peter replies: 'The Messiah of God.'

It is clear that Peter has hit the nail on the head. Jesus is not one of the prophets, but the one who sums up all of God's promises.

Yet, Jesus throws us once again by sternly warning the disciples not to say anything to anyone. The word used here is the same one Luke put on the Master's lips when he shouted at the spirit of the unclean demon not to speak, to be silent (cf. Lk 4:35). We can intuit a rather strong emotion, then, in Jesus: how come that on the one hand he wants the people to gradually come to know him and then, at a certain point, he takes a step back? Jesus appears to explain it in the following words: 'The Son of Man must undergo great suffering, and be rejected by the elders, Chief priests, and scribes, and be killed, and on the third day be raised' (v. 22).

We are faced with a complex set of elements.

We will look first of all at why Jesus is presented to us as someone who is stopping them from speaking; we will deduce the reason from the other Gospels.

The expression, 'the Messiah (or Christ) of God' immediately stirs up a range of emotions and messianic hopes, the hopes that this Christ would take the situation in hand and set in motion the final solution to all the problems. A certain concept of Messiah is understood here.

Instead, what is being proposed here is a markedly different figure: *the Christ will be crushed.* How is this possible? Here we have a very serious problem for the apostles' grasp of things, for Judaism, for the first converts. The Christ must suffer much: Luke clearly means death by these words, and this is confirmed by the Greek term that is translated as 'be rejected' in English.

It is a tremendous *scandal* because the ones who reject him have intelligence, are rulers, have responsibility, are individuals whom people trust, and are the support for all the simple people of Israel. These individuals will reject him, will fail him in the examination of his credentials, will not accept him. This is certainly an inconceivable thing if we consider that Jesus came and lived among his people. The disciples struggle to understand the rejection in a figurative sense and do not accept that Jesus' destiny should culminate in being put to death.

After this episode, Jesus goes on to say: 'If any want to become my followers, let them deny themselves and take up their cross daily and follow me' (Lk 9:23).

The figurative language resumes here but the disciples understand little and at a superficial level, without succeeding in assimilating what they hear. In reality, in both his preaching on the Passion and the discourse to follow, Jesus wanted to teach that he is referring to committed Christian life as a life of renunciation, that there

113

is no mission without involvement and this involvement can extend to extreme, paradoxical cases, even to the point of eliminating the very possibility of pursuing the mission. The hand that is offered is not only rejected but cut off, and that is the scandal of the offer Jesus makes of himself. Nevertheless, the words remain hanging and we are told nothing about the disciples' reactions.

Betrayed into human hands: Luke 9:43-45

We move on to the prediction that follows:

1) What is the context? It is a context of enthusiasm and amazement resulting from the miraculous healing of the boy tormented by an unclean spirit and whom the disciples were unable to heal; Jesus heals him, the people celebrate him and everyone is astounded at the greatness of God.

2) Just when the apostles have proof of Jesus' power before their eyes he tells them: 'Let these words sink into your ears: *The Son of Man is going to be betrayed into human hands.*'

Once more an enigmatic statement, one that, however, underlines another aspect of the awareness he has of his mission. Meanwhile, it is clear from the text that Jesus wants to emphasise the words ('Let these words sink in') because they are very important. 'The Son of Man is going to be betrayed into human hands.'

The prophecy is closer at hand than it was in the previous prediction: there, it was in the future; here, the betrayal of the Son of Man is already imminent. The reference is clearly to something sinister because the Son of Man will no longer be in control of himself but in the power of others who will dispose of him; he came into the world to restore everything and instead will be at the mercy of others.

We can now start to deepen our prayer before the Lord and endeavour to enter into Jesus' mind and heart. He defines himself – this, in fact is his definition – as the one 'betrayed into human hands.' Jesus will accomplish it to the extent of the Eucharist where he betrays himself into human hands, running the risk that they will abuse him. We call this folly, this placing of oneself into anyone else's hands, trusting that person to do whatever they want for good or for evil. However, Jesus offers himself as good, available, merciful – ready to share our circumstances to the point of placing himself in our hands.

3) Luke emphasises in the strongest way possible the fact that the apostles understand nothing of this, repeating the idea three times: 'But they did not understand this saying: its meaning was concealed from them, so that they could not perceive it and they were afraid to ask him about this saying' (Lk 9:45).

Luke has never stressed a concept to such an extent and if we try to give the terms he has used better consideration, we will gain an even clearer idea of the impact he means to give this episode.

'They did not understand': the Greek verb means to not recognise, to disown the words and is the same term used to indicate that the leaders of the people did not recognise God's justice, had not understood his plan and were prepared to practise their own justice. It is also the verb that expresses the condemnation we find in the *First Letter to the Corinthians* where Paul writes: 'Anyone who does not recognises this is not to be recognised' (1 Cor 14:38).

God will not recognise someone who fails to recognise his salvific plan.

We are faced with an *incapacity to receive God's plan* by people (the disciples) who have completed their internship in Jesus' company, a training in enthusiasm and discipleship, yet they are still blind. Luke insists, because what Jesus is saying is so very important, inasmuch as it specifies really *how* he is the Christ: by giving himself and handing himself over. These words that defined the Paschal Mystery were like a veil before their eyes and bring to mind the Book of the Apocalypse, the revelation of the hidden mystery that only God can reveal and concerning which only God can open our eyes.

The apostles, then, still have their eyes closed. Luke adds: 'Its meaning was concealed from them, so that they could not perceive it.'

They heard with their ears but they lacked the deep perception of the situation, and moreover were afraid to ask Jesus. A situation of ambiguity was created, one we so often find in ourselves, in our communities and everyday life: we see that something is less than clear, yet just the same we fear clarification, we fear knowing the real situation, and do not want to go into it.

This fear can be an unconscious one, and in prayer we wish to ask that we can overcome it, know better how to face up to things we are not well-disposed to accepting; it is a little like the fear of the seriously ill person who prefers not to learn more about the illness, afraid of being unable to bear the truth.

It is an essential problem for the disciples, since this is about the Jesus they have dedicated their lives to. Yet they prefer not to ask, to remain in the dark.

'Lord, can we put the ultimate question to you and ourselves? Lord, help us understand what we are afraid to ask, and above all, help us recognise that the mystery of the cross is hidden, and as much as we might speak of it and exercise ourselves about it, it remains invisible to our human eyes. Only the Holy Spirit can transform us and allow us to grasp it in practice, even though our weakness hides it from us so much that recognising it will always be a surprise, every time.'

At any rate, the apostles still have to take the whole journey to Jerusalem with Jesus, a journey during which Jesus will propose in word and deed a very exalted message (that includes the Passion, the meaning of the cross, freedom of heart, detachment, total abandonment to the Father), and will give them the opportunity to verify what stage they are at in following him. Who could ever have offered a better school?

The Scriptures will be fulfilled: Luke 18:31-34

Luke wants to tell us what the situation is at the end of the journey.

———

117

By now they are near Jericho, and taking the Twelve aside, Jesus explains: 'See, we are going up to Jerusalem, and everything that is written about the Son of Man by the prophets will be accomplished.'

We note a new element. Earlier the expression 'must happen' or 'is about to happen' indicated the divine will in general terms. Now it is said that the Scriptures 'will be accomplished,' that we are at the culminating point of the plan of salvation. How is such a moment described? The Son of Man 'will be handed over to the Gentiles: and he will be mocked, and insulted and spat upon. After they have flogged him they will kill him, and on the third day he will rise again. But they understood nothing about all these things; in fact, what he said was hidden from them, and they did not grasp what was said' (vv. 32-34).

Other than recalling the Scriptures on fulfilment of the divine plan, there are other hints that show how Luke sees the Passion: Jesus will be handed over to the Gentiles, thus rejected in such a way that his fellow citizens would not even need to get their hands dirty. They would put him into the hands of people who did not honour God and he would be thrown away like something Israel didn't want to know about. Emphasis is placed especially on the humiliations: he would be made fun of, mocked, despised; they would spit on him (this aspect of personal humiliation of a human being is specified). He would be 'handed over' and this would ensure not only ill-treatment but being vilified as a human being. Then after being flogged they would kill him. This mention of flogging is interesting. Luke will omit it in his specific account of the Passion.

'On the third day he will rise again.' This is the point of arrival that was missing in the second prediction. It is clear that Jesus makes this explicit so we can contemplate the whole picture; and the apostles, who cannot understand the Passion, do not understand the resurrection either. We could ask: why don't they at least rejoice at the final goal? Because they *do not see* what is about to happen, so Luke concludes: 'But they understood nothing about all these things.'

The Greek word translated as 'not understand' occurs a number of times in Luke's and Mark's Gospels, always in situations where the mystery is not understood: 'Do you still not perceive or understand? Are your hearts hardened? Do you have eyes and fail to see? Do you have ears and fail to hear? And do you not remember?' (Mk 8:17-18).

It is the same word that is found in the context of the mysterious preaching of the parables: 'They will hear and will not understand.'

The mystery of Christ, the Paschal Mystery, is hidden from human eyes and only God can make it understood.

The problem, in Luke 18, becomes so serious that some exegetes prefer to believe that Luke and Mark are speaking of anticipated predictions and explain the surprise at Jesus' death and the disciples' flight in this way.

It does not seem to be a good solution to me, not even from a psychological point of view; we know very well in fact that there are things that we *do not want* to understand.

That goes for Luke, especially in the second and third predictions. Jesus understood what he was heading toward and expressed it; however, his disciples were not inclined to understand it. It is the fundamental fact on which the Evangelist wants to make us reflect: Jesus knew what was about to happen, felt that it was bound up with his mission, that it was the consequence of his giving himself as the good and defenceless Word, offering himself with love. He understood it and sought to explain it to his disciples with veiled hints, but to no avail.

We have to conclude, then, that after the instruction the evangelical disciple has received, his capacity to discern is non-existent.

This mystery of *incomprehension* moves and disturbs us: if the apostles have not understood, not even will we be able to understand, and we need to ask the Lord who died and is risen that his mystery may penetrate our lives. We will not get anywhere through our reasoning, in terms of really accepting it, because it would involve us too much. Unfortunately, we have an extreme capacity for limiting or dodging such involvement, even though we say we accept it.

'Lord, help us to understand what we do not accept, what we discard, leave in the shade, always dodging around it without wanting to tackle it.'

When we say, 'This point is not open for discussion' and we say it with some emotion, it is clear that it is a sore point and anything else said is an attempt to dodge the real sticking point, requiring us to compromise ourselves, lose something. This is how the disciples behaved: 'This is not for you! Messiah, yes, but to go through this trial, no.'

It is not enough to focus our gaze on glory. We need to fix our gaze on the face of him who suffered and has been made perfect and achieved glory (cf. Heb 5:8-9). It is only in prolonged prayer that the dark areas in us can emerge, the deep-seated refusal we bear and that we have filed away, so to speak. And then we will ask ourselves if perhaps our weak point, our paschal mystery, our 'passing over' to the Lord in death, does not lie there in some of these dark areas – in the certainty that Jesus will help us to never lose sight of the ultimate object of our life of faith, which is himself.

Prayer becomes a kind of admission into death, a total opening of oneself to God's word in the desire that no part of us remains in darkness, that the Word may enlighten us and burn up any impurity in us. Adoration and praise of God who saves us, in the certain confidence of his grace, is the place of our peace, our life, our resurrection.

'Lord Jesus, you know that like the apostles we seek at any cost to reject the truth of your difficult message and do not know how to follow you and where you are going. We imagine that following you is easy, exultant, and we reject what you prepare for us every day.

Enlighten our mind, warm our heart so we can understand what you want of us. You see, this talk about your Passion is in itself already difficult for us in our everyday experiences. Help us at least to see that if we go more deeply into these experiences we will discover what it is you want of us: that is, our poor offering to you, weak and lukewarm as it is. Make us capable, Lord, of being accepted by you. May we accept you completely without hiding anything from you.

Virgin Mary, you assented perfectly to God's word and allowed yourself to be moulded and transformed by the Word to the point of complete giving yourself beneath the cross. With the apostles, you enjoyed the fullness of the Holy Spirit given to the Church. Obtain for us the grace of following the life of your Son in truth. Reveal to each of us what this truth consists of, and help us live joyfully.'

2

THE TRUE MEANING OF THE CROSS

'Lord Jesus, you did not want to spare your Mother her painful and dramatic participation in your suffering. Help us also to share in it in some way. Warm our cold and distant hearts so they can experience, with Mary, your death for us.

Mother of Jesus, help us to grasp the true meaning of the cross, and may this meaning shine forth in our prayer, in our difficulties, in our contact with the sufferings of others. Give us the right attitude to the sufferings of the world and people everywhere. May we pray with you, Mother of Jesus, in union with the sufferings of all humanity.'

The grace to ask for in this meditation is indicated by the title: the true meaning of the cross, a title we could be more specific about: myself, Peter and the cross. Jesus' cross is his experience of the outward failure of his mission and the opposition that leads him to his death. Peter represents the chosen disciple who followed him on his journey, and we approach him in order to see and experience the cross from his point of view, meditating on Peter's drama so we can also understand our own.

In fact, in Peter we can read our reaction before the cross. He is not only the chosen disciple: he is the simple, sincere human being without ulterior motives, who takes things as they are, reacts to them according to his own sensitivities and is surprisingly carried forward. We will follow him on the journey until the culminating point, his situation during the Lord's Passion (Lk 22:62). It is a culminating moment but not the final one: the final moment is the proclamation of Luke 25:34: 'The Lord has risen indeed and he has appeared to Simon.'

Cross and conversion

We are reflecting on a complex theme in which we encounter so many realities: Christ's cross, our cross, the crosses of other people, the world's cross, the consolation we can offer. Everything is complicated by the shades of meaning the problem assumes for each of us by virtue of our experience, our sharing in the sufferings of our brothers and sisters. We are before a very personal element: the endless forms of prayer there are (our prayer is ours and no one else's), and thus the endless ways of confronting, feeling, experiencing the cross, and everyone has their own. On the one hand, then, we feel defenceless when speaking, and on the other, we see the urgent need to encourage ourselves to seek the grace, our own state of prayer, to confront our own sufferings and the sufferings of others, in truth. This will be the fruit of meditation.

One of the obstacles hindering the emergence of the truth of ourselves in our experience of the cross and in others' experience of it, is the intellectual gaps we have in the theological question of redemption. It is a difficult topic for which theology has devised a range of explanations that have little satisfied us and have not helped us to clarify the mystery as we would have hoped. Rather, perhaps, they have obscured it and made it ponderous. This is the difficulty with theologies born, not of lived experience of conversion and the cross, but abstract considerations. We must also free ourselves, if there is need to, of certain claims that abstract theologies have affected us with, regarding the theme of cross, sacrifice, self-denial and all connected issues, such as the victory over sensuality and the topic of sexuality itself. For example, I have encountered, in an American writer, a total inability to understand the meaning of celibacy and hence the total absence of the meaning of the cross, combined with an odd and suspect permissiveness. Once certain basic elements have been discarded from our spiritual life, we are no longer able to see where we will end up.

When conversion is not deeply anchored in the lived gospel and problems are examined in the abstract, the consequences can be harmful. This is why we are invited especially to develop within ourselves the profound, true, lived meaning of evangelical conversion and to tackle the realities of the Christian life as we experience it, so we can then ask theology to enlighten such realities, and not vice versa.

The reality of the evangelical life that we read of in the Scriptures and the lives of the saints, cannot be conditioned by constructed theories and ways of thinking that do not begin from an authentic adult faith.

We see, then, how delicate the topic is that we are dealing with and the many resonances it may have for our way of understanding life, the apostolate, asceticism, self-denial.

Myself, Peter and the cross

Of itself, Luke's Gospel is not the best manual for meditation on Peter's journey, given that Luke spares the apostle a good deal (it is Mark who presents the drama well and reports Jesus' rebukes in a robust fashion). For example, in Luke we do not find Peter's remonstration with Jesus after the first prediction of the Passion, and the word 'Satan' which the Lord calls him.

Again, Luke does not speak of Peter as the one who was asleep in Gethsemane and to whom Jesus turns regretfully. Even the words, 'Put your sword back in its scabbard' that John refers to as directed to Peter, are not reported. Furthermore, in order to show his friend in a good light, only Luke gives us the sentence: 'I have prayed for you that your own faith may not fail' (22:31), while Peter's boastfulness at the Last Supper ('Even though they all become deserters, I will not,') is omitted.

So, he spares Peter, leaves him in the shade. But we will meditate on the basis of Luke, though bearing Mark and John in mind.

We will begin by reflecting on Luke 9:20 to see especially the beginning of Peter's journey regarding the way of the cross. Then we will move on to considering Peter at the Last Supper, Peter in the Garden of Gethsemane, Peter in the courtyard during Jesus' Passion.

Providing for the kingdom

In Luke 9:20 we see Peter at a culminating moment of his career when he feels satisfied because he has said what the others were unable to say: 'You are the Messiah of God.' The trust shown him by the Master right from the time he was called meant that he had been made to feel and perceive that he was to have an important mission. Now he is at the height of joy, believing the mission has been conferred on him: it is he, after all, who proclaimed 'the Messiah of God,' the Christ, and gave voice to what was timid and implicit in the others. He has had the courage and shown Jesus in a good light. We can imagine the suffering and humiliation when immediately afterwards Jesus dampens the enthusiasm and forbids them to talk about this, while he begins to speak about the cross.

Let us listen to Mark 8:32. Peter is troubled by the announcement of the Passion, feels the need to remonstrate with Jesus and tells him: 'No, this is not for you.' The only result he gains is to strongly irritate the Master.

Let us try to imagine that it is Peter telling the story and ask him what was going on at that moment. He would probably tell us he no longer understood anything: 'I had lifted the Lord's spirits, praised him and no way could I allow him to go to the cross. I wanted to spare him the cross because I respected him and had great affection for him. I wanted him to understand that we sinners would have been ready to suffer instead of him. Then the Lord began shouting at me and railing against me and I no longer understood anything. So, I shut up and asked myself: who, then, is this Jesus?'

And really, in the episode that immediately followed the Transfiguration, Peter had not understood the lesson. There he wanted once again to look after the Master and exclaimed: 'Master, it is good for us to be here; let us make three dwellings, one for you, one for Moses and one for Elijah.' Luke adds: 'not knowing what he said' (9:33).

Let us try to put ourselves into the scene: convinced that we have to provide for Jesus and his guests, it is almost as if we are saying, 'Let us look after this, now we are here.'

Note Peter's generosity: the dwellings (tents) are for Jesus, Moses and Eijah, while the apostles will be left in the open. Peter, however, feels he is at the heart of the scene and maybe he will come down from the mountain still with this trust in himself.

Further on, the Evangelist tells us that the apostles who were left behind down below had not been able to cast the devil out of a boy (cf. Lk 9:27-40). Perhaps Peter would have looked at them with a certain smugness due to their failed exorcism, saying to himself, in Jesus' words: 'You faithless generation!'

Deep down, Peter's psychology is ours. He felt he had been invested with the kingdom and was truly capable of doing great things, looking after it like Jesus and maybe even a bit better than him. This attitude becomes part of us when what we do – even in the church – becomes so much part of our identity that we consider our work, and our apostolate precisely 'ours' more than the Lord's.

Self-sufficiency

We move on without there being much progress (because Luke emphasises how the apostles, hence also Peter, had understood nothing of the predictions of the Passion) to the Last Supper episode, particularly in Luke 22:31-34.

We note above all the repetition of the name, twice – this also happens when he is chiding Martha in Luke 10:41 – that indicates the seriousness of the situation as well as Jesus' real affection:

> 'Simon, Simon, listen! Satan has demand-ed to sift all of you like wheat, but I have prayed for you that your own faith may not fail; and you, once you have turned back, strengthen your brothers.' And he said to him, 'Lord, I am ready to go with you to prison and to death!' Jesus said, 'I tell you, Peter, the cock will not crow this day until you have denied three times that you know me!'

Let us try to put ourselves in Peter's shoes as he is challenged in such a heartfelt and loving way: 'Simon, Simon.'

He is the object of Jesus' loving rebuke: 'Peter, you do not grasp the real situation. You are not in the right and do not understand what is going on around us. You are so full of yourself and your ability to do something for me that you almost consider yourself my benefactor, my saviour. I have prayed for you because it is you who need my prayer. Your faith is at risk. I have prayed for you so that you may then be able to help the others, but only when you turn back.' And here there is a very gentle hint: 'Look, you are teetering on the abyss, you are on the edge. While you believe you are helping me carry the cross, you are about to be crushed by it.'

Peter replies with beautiful words: 'Lord, I am ready to go *with you*.' What more could he say? The expression of St Ignatius in the *Spiritual Exercises* comes to mind: 'Whoever wants to come with me must work with me so that by following me in suffering he will also follow me in joy.'

But these words, as beautiful as they are, count for nothing. How come Peter has erred? Probably because he is even abusing some of the Lord's words. He had just been told: 'I have prayed for you,' and, instead of drawing knowledge of his poverty and fragility from it, Peter finds a reason for self-sufficiency and presumption. He has not grasped the hint about turning back, the risk to his faith; only the hint about himself whom the kingdom of God has need of ('Strengthen your brothers'). He doesn't even need the Lord to pray for him because he is sure he can do it alone. Jesus replies: 'Look, Peter, the catastrophe is imminent.' And he continues to not understand, along with the other apostles, so much so that immediately after saying 'I am ready to go with you to prison and to death' in v. 38, as soon as the swords are seen, these words acquire another meaning. We read this between the lines even if it is not written in the text: 'Here are two swords, we are ready to die, but in your defence, Lord. We want to defend you. We want to make you see that we are capable of looking after you.'

It is a complete reversal of the gospel, where it is not Jesus who saves us but we who save him and his Church; it is no longer a gospel of divine initiative but the gospel of our brilliance in acting on behalf of God.

When the two swords come to light, Peter felt his real manliness come to the fore, the man who wants to do something for the Lord, because he never succeeded in accepting that Jesus was more generous than he was, that he was at Jesus' service and that he should allow himself to be led. Peter has always translated everything into self-sufficiency, so did not understand Jesus' teaching on salvation for the poor, the need for conversion of the sinner. Even when he declared, 'I am a sinner' (Lk 5:8), he said it to take up his power once more and fool himself regarding his possibilities.

Passion

And so, we come to the Garden of Olives (vv. 39-46).

We have already stressed how Peter is spared by Luke, so we will let Mark help us. However, also reading Luke we contemplate Jesus at prayer, in agony, and sweating blood. We then ask ourselves: Where is Peter? Why isn't he there? We also ask this of ourselves since we would have behaved like him. Personally, I confess I would have been frightened by Jesus' anguish, and would not have wanted to see him weeping. I would have drawn aside out of a sense of protection and affection. I would have been unable to look at him in that state of depression.

So, Peter is afraid of Jesus' anguish and does not know how to find the right words; he prefers to remain apart, eliminate the scene he refuses to absorb, and allows himself to sleep out of the grief of which Luke speaks (Lk 22:45).

We all know from experience that it is difficult to bear the pain of a person dear to us when we are impotent to help; perhaps we can bear it to the point where we feel useful and important, but when the suffering reveals our incapacity and inadequacy, we prefer to withdraw, fear being caught up in the feelings and emotions we are unable to master. Peter sees that he cannot control Jesus' anguish precisely because his way of understanding the gospel prevents him from doing so. This reveals the false notion of salvation that Peter has not yet fully eliminated. He feels lost in the presence of his Master's sorrow, and he certainly begins to crumble.

He would have wanted to be with Jesus as far as prison, the cross, but in circumstances he could deal with in a virile manner, with courage and with sword in hand. Now instead, when faced with Jesus' temptation and humiliation, he is once more devastated. The final blow to his certainty we read in v. 46: Jesus says to them – to Peter, according to Mark and everyone, according to Luke – 'Why are you sleeping? Get up and pray that you may not come into the time of trial.'

Jesus clearly sees that these men have a weak, obscure, confused faith and are about to be over-whelmed. He encourages them: 'Pray', that is, place yourself in the real situation of being God's beggars. Do not stop to think about how to exercise your ability to react, but confess the truth of the moment, what Jesus is confessing in his words: 'Father, I will not get through this without your strength; I would prefer not to drink this cup.' Jesus himself is praying and humbly stating the truth of human weakness; nevertheless, the disciples do not accept such weakness.

They sleep, knowing that prayer will only lead them to discover their misery, to recognise it, recognise their need to be saved, more than Jesus' need. This is why they come into temptation; the falsehood they are left in overwhelms them.

All this emerges in the capture scene (Lk 24:47 ff.). The situation changes rapidly – the crowd and Judas enter, emotions run high.

What does Peter do? He wants to save Jesus and has recourse to the sword, and his manliness takes over: 'The Master must not die. We have to defend him!'

Let us ask Peter: 'What did you think you were doing by this gesture?' and he replies: 'I wanted to prevent Jesus from dying at the expense of my life; I could not accept his being captured, but I would have accepted them capturing me. I lost my head and was ready to cut off someone else's. Just as well the blow missed and I avoided something worse.'

Jesus opposes him and at this point Peter loses all his courage and asks himself: 'What can I do, then? What does the Master want from me? I have deeply compromised myself and now he orders me to turn back and even mercifully heals the man with the injured ear. I no longer understand a thing; evidently I am useless.'

Rebuffed by Jesus, humiliated and confused, Peter is at the peak of temptation.

There is still a final word from Jesus that sweeps away all security: 'But this is your hour, and the power of darkness!'

I imagine Peter would have thought: 'But if he didn't even resist the power of darkness, where will we end up? If he accepts the power of darkness over himself, can we know what will happen? Whatever is this kingdom he spoke so much about?'

For Peter, the disappointment is enormous, complete: 'Not only am I prevented from helping him but I don't even know what role I'm supposed to play!'

The apostle has lost his identity.

Letting himself be loved

Nevertheless, since he is good and sincere and Jesus has prayed for him, Peter does not want to completely abandon the Master, and he follows him, with love, even though very discouraged. He continues to think about what will happen and deep down hopes he can still help him, be of use to him.

In this state of mind, more with feelings of affection than conviction, he follows Jesus. We are finally witnessing Peter's truth explode. It had already shown up in his poverty in Gethsemane. He has fallen fully and is forced to publicly recognise his total bewilderment.

———

In Gethsemane he could still carry things off with a degree of glory, but now he hears with his own ears the point he has come to.

Let us consider the questions put to him.

A servant-girl sees him sitting by the fire, looks at him and says: 'This man was also with him' (Lk 22:56).

How beautiful are those words, 'with him!' They are the same used by Peter: 'with you', but he denies it, saying, 'I do not know him!'

How true this statement is. It underlines Peter's bitterness, but not what he was thinking: 'That man has disappointed me. I cannot understand him, I no longer know him.' They express his fear and disappointment, his bewilderment: 'I no longer know what to say about him.'

At v. 58, comes Peter's second public humiliation. Someone else accuses him: 'You also are one of them!'

The first question queried his relationship with Jesus, the second with the disciples. He replies, thinking the others have run off: 'Man, I am not!'

He is even unable to refer to his friends whom he possibly thinks are different from himself at this moment because they are not around. He has lost the meaning of the relationship with the Lord and the community of his brothers: by denying one he denies the others.

Luke continues: 'about an hour later.' What a terrible hour! What happened to you in that hour, Peter? 'It was the most fearful hour of my life: lost, eaten up with remorse, fear, the inability to pick myself up again, not knowing what I had to do or who I was.'

———

Words he had heard previously must have echoed in him like a hammer in his head: 'And I tell you, everyone who acknowledges me before others, the Son of Man will also acknowledge before the angels of God; but whoever denies me before others will be denied before the angels of God' (Lk 12:8-9).

Peter is devastated by these words that come and go in him, disturbing him. And he hears once more another of the Master's teachings: 'When they bring you before the synagogues, the rulers, and the authorities, do not worry about how you are to defend yourself or what you are to say; for the Holy Spirit will teach you at that very hour what you ought to say' (Lk 12:11-12).

With what shame, instead, does Peter see that he has entered precisely into that temptation; he is confused and bewildered. He is worried about himself, his own role, how he should deal with things since it is up to him to save Jesus, Jesus who had not let himself be saved.

In such confusion and humiliation, we read the final question, the most insistent one: 'Surely this man was also with him, for he is a Galilean?' But Peter said: 'Man I do not know what you are talking about!' (Lk 2:59-60).

Peter is completely unmasked. Luke uses the same expression employed in the account of the Transfiguration regarding the three tents: 'not knowing what he said' (Lk 9:34).

Peter has allowed the truth of himself to emerge, let his poverty show up, and has come to the point of no longer understanding himself. The situation is completely out of hand; he is lost and does not know what to do, what is expected of him. The only feeling he has is the instinct to save his skin, not compromise himself, and then he's had enough. The time has come when there is nothing more worth doing.

So, not even the cock crowing (v. 60) makes an impact. It is the accusation of sin, a cold, cutting accusation but the apostle does not understand its meaning. 'At that moment ... the cock crowed. The Lord turned and looked at Peter. Then Peter remembered the word of the Lord, how he had said to him, "Before the cock crows today, you will deny me three times." And he went out and wept bitterly' (v. 61).

Let us ask Peter what happened at that moment and why Jesus' look opened his eyes, revealing to him the truth of the whole situation. He would have more or less thought: 'He is dying for me, worm and coward that I am (here is the truth!); I wanted to be someone and now he is dying for me, poor man that I am, reduced to not knowing who I am. You have conquered me, Lord; you are better than me; I thought I could succeed, do something for you, but you have overcome me with your goodness. You are going to die for me and I am ashamed of myself.'

The first expression of Peter's conversion had been: 'Go away from me, Lord, for I am a sinful man' (Lk 5:8).

Now he compares himself with the Lord's love, and finally understands that Jesus loves him and asks him to let himself be loved.

The scales have fallen from Peter's eyes and he acknowledges that he had always refused to let himself be loved, had always refused to allow himself to be fully saved by Jesus and so did not want the Lord to love him fully. But Jesus' extraordinary greatness consists precisely in dying for him and he must accept this love, incredible though it is!

How difficult it is to let ourselves be loved, really loved! We always want a part of ourselves not to be tied to recognition, while in reality we are in debt totally because God is supreme and saves us totally, with love.

The conclusion of Peter's journey is in Luke 24:34: 'The Lord has risen indeed and he has appeared to Simon.'

In personal meditation, let us seek to ask Peter what difference had taken place between Jesus' look and the appearance of the Risen Lord. Fundamentally, already in that look he had understood that he was infinitely loved and all the rest became clear to him: Jesus is love, life, God; his death is a death out of love and can only be on behalf of life. Therefore, the resurrection was already included in that look of acceptance.

What does Peter feel when the Risen Lord makes himself present? I think he experiences immense joy for Jesus. By now it is only the Lord who counts for Peter, so his consolation is the same as Jesus' consolation, a consolation poured over him, overwhelming him and in which all the rest is immersed. Opening himself to being loved is acceptance without limits of the Lord's consolation in the resurrection; not the worried, exhausting consolation we strive to achieve at times, but the consolation of someone who allows himself to be swept up by God's plan and because of which Christ's glory becomes his glory. Let us ask Peter that we may share in his experience and in the true meaning of the cross.

Jesus, you permitted Peter to go through so many fears so the truth of the gospel would shine forth in him, the gospel truth he was to manifest to others. Help us also to let ourselves be loved in all our trials. May we recognise your goodness, allow ourselves to be conquered by your love so we may know you as you are, the God who loves us. And may we be able to joyfully share in your glory and proclaim it to others. You who live and reign forever and ever. Amen.'

3

MARY'S CROSS

'We adore you, Lord, in the memory of your Mother's sorrows. Grant us the grace, Lord, to be able to remember you with faith, humility and affection.

Virgin Mary, Mother of Jesus and our Mother, you know how fragile our love is and perhaps this is why it is difficult to speak to you. In our attempt to do so, grant us your protection, your help, your kindness and patience, your contentment with the little we can say. Enlighten us and accept us as we are. See that we are received by the love of your Son, who lives and reigns forever and ever. Amen.'

In meditating on Mary's cross, we need to repeat what we have observed regarding prayer and the cross: the relationship each of us has with the Mother of Jesus is as varied and manifold as the stages of our spiritual development. Above all, the expression of this relationship changes in accordance with our spiritual and emotional education.

In this regard, we should emphasise that beginning with Vatican Council II, this emotional and spiritual education has decreased, or we are less inclined socially or collectively to live and express our spiritual rapport with the Mother of

Jesus. Because of this, too, it is probably difficult to speak about it and display it even though it may be alive and deep in our heart.

On the other hand, it seems to me to be appropriate to reflect on Mary and the cross, associating ourselves with her (myself, Mary and the cross), and seeing in Mary the disciple who wants to make our journey. She understood it much more intimately and suffered much more subtly than Peter did, so she can help introduce us to it.

However, given that the episode of Mary at the foot of the cross is almost indescribable, I thought of beginning from the beginning as Luke does in his preface: 'I too, decided after investigating everything very carefully from the very first, to write an orderly account for you …' (1:3).

Now the mystery of Mary is really a mystery of origins.

Hence, we go back to the source of the mystery to meditate on the events that prepared for the coming of the Son of God into the world, events that Luke describes with greater precision and intensity. Let us consider first of all the mystery of preparation (about which Luke offers the most texts); then the early enthusiasm (as a specific moment of the preparation); then the dark moments; and finally, we will contemplate Mary beneath the cross and Mary in the Church.

Mary's journey winds between two extremes: the first at Nazareth and the other with the apostles in the Upper Room. Her experience of the Paschal Mystery finds its culminating moment beneath the cross, even if Luke does not record the episode and passes directly to presenting us with Mary in the Church.

The mystery of the preparation

I restrict myself to emphasising elements pertaining to Mary's sharing in the cross so we can grasp, through this specific piece of the action, how she is moulded by God.

Let us fix our attention on the account of the Annunciation, where we find three particularly pertinent comments of Luke's (1:29, 34, 38):

1) 'But she was much perplexed by his words and pondered what sort of greeting this might be' (v. 29).

The original Greek term translated by 'was much perplexed' is very strong in itself: it indicates real agitation, deep inner confusion. For example, it is the same fear that overcame Herod when the Magi were with him and he became aware that something new and big was about to take place that could upset his plans (cf. Mt 2:3). Mary was devout, resolute, generous and saw that God was intervening to disturb her calm, was entering her life as an upsetting element.

The verb is used by Luke in Chapter 1:12: Zachariah discovers that God is upsetting the well-established and tranquil habit of his old age.

We find another typical case in Matthew 14:26 when Jesus walks on water and the disciples are confounded when they see him.

What happens in Mary when she *ponders* what God's power will achieve in her regard (the verb 'ponder' indicates a kind of inward debate, deep reflection)? She knows it is risky to be touched by such power, knows that it changes the destiny of those it touches, like the fate of Jeremiah and the other prophets. Although she fully abandons herself to the mystery she has an awareness, typical of the Bible, that God comes in order to confound. This is already an announcement of the cross in Mary's life, when she allows herself to be seized by God's confounding action.

2) It seems to be that the same sentiment returns at v. 34: 'How can this be, since I am a virgin?'

Mary has a direction and choice of her own but she perceives that the divine power wants to change her situation. She does not know how but she is certain that it will operate for her good and the good of the world, even if she recognises that her personal existence is now out of her hands. She offers herself and her good resolve.

3) Finally in v. 38, the answer that sums up the mystery of Mary very well: 'Here I am, the servant of the Lord; let it be with me according to your word.'

Luke, in a desire to go to the root 'of the events that have taken place among us', sees in these words the source of all that will happen.

The expression: 'Here I am, the servant of the Lord', indicates total trust and is somewhat harsh. Our mind goes back to the song of the psalmist: 'as the eyes of a maid to the hand of her mistress' (Ps 123 [122]: 2); what the mistress commands or says, be it life or death, must be done.

Mary's life, then, is entrusted to the will of God who can take her and do with her what he wants. This attitude includes full awareness that the Lord has the right to a person's life, has the right for good or for ill.

We can reflect on Mary's state of prayer: from the moment of the Annunciation hers is a prayer of unlimited trust. We will see, nevertheless, that she must still be amazed, still suffer, because emotionally not all is complete. Her prayer will take on hues of suffering and bitterness, perhaps of disappointment, at least as a mother, in order to be faithful to her resolve.

'Let it be with me according to your word'; I would not interpret these words as a second prayer, repeating the first, but rather a wish. Mary has already entered joyfully into what was announced to her and she hopes it will come about. She has happily and serenely ratified what the Lord has given her to understand.

Early enthusiasm

The very same joyousness is expressed a little later.

Once seized by God's power, at the beginning she enjoys the wonderful fruit of this power, and her joy explodes during the moment of the Visitation, in praise received and returned.

Mary receives praise: 'Blessed are you among women and blessed is the fruit of your womb!' (v. 42).

There can be no greater greeting for a mother; it is the height of exultation since God has produced in her what will make her blessed, his own Son. God could not give her more than that. As well as being the Mother of the Lord (1:43), she brings joy to John (1:44) and is blessed for her faith (1:45).

It is interesting to note, in the praises that come to Elizabeth's lips, the frank and open nature of the Scripture, unafraid to offer praise. Perhaps we so often use the word 'humility' incorrectly, forgetting that it is simply the recognition of the truth; in this case, the truth of the matter is stated. The time will come when Mary must suffer humiliation and loneliness. Now, however, God's truth is expressed through Elizabeth who proclaims: Blessed are *you*, blessed are you *who believed*, you the *Mother of the Lord*, you who *bring joy to* our home.

And Mary replies with the simplicity of someone who returns the praise to its origin: 'My soul magnifies the Lord' (v. 46).

The *Magnificat* is the evangelical song *par excellence.* In it is God's greatness, God's praise, our poverty; God who confounds human existence and changes destinies, the merciful and compassionate God who comes to our aid. The gospel is already a reality for Mary and her response is perfectly evangelical. She does not speak explicitly of suffering, however her song hints at it and also gives it meaning. The suffering is not terminal but abandonment to God's power. God intervenes in human events, inserting himself through this confounding, because he loves us and wishes to enrich our poverty with his fullness.

Let us ask Mary to give us this evangelical spirit from which comes the possibility of understanding the cross, the spirit of praise and recognition of God's greatness. Let us ask her to teach us to frame everything within the divine and merciful initiative that nothing can escape from.

Dark moments

The dark moments soon begin:

1) It seems strange that Luke does not describe, at least minimally, Mary's state of mind in the account of the birth and the facts surrounding Jesus. She is simply the Mother who brings him into the world and places him in the manger. While elation, joy, angels and shepherds are there, Mary is there in her function as a mother, and the only thing said of her is: 'Mary treasured all these words and pondered them in her heart' (2:19).

What is going on in her and how does she view these events?

Mary is experiencing inner growth, predisposed by God. As a mother, she should feel she is at the centre of events; in reality the events demonstrate to her right from the outset that her Son will be leaving her and is greater than her. Immediately she is set aside because heaven, earth and people she did not invite arrive and congratulate the Son, not the mother, as usually happens at a birth. The Son is the centre of attention and interest, so Mary, in her immense joy as a mother, receives a warning: it is he alone who counts for something. From this moment on she learns to do everything for Jesus even returning into obscurity.

We can see this in the infancy episodes that follow.

2) During the Presentation in the Temple, Simeon contemplates Jesus and exclaims: 'This child is destined for the falling and rising of many in Israel, and to be a sign that will be opposed, so that the inner thoughts of many will

be revealed – and a sword will pierce your own soul too' (Lk 2:35).

It is difficult for us to determine what this 'sword' means for Mary. Naturally we immediately think of the cross, however it is Luke who records this episode and he does not show us Mary beneath the cross. So if we want to correctly interpret the meaning of the 'sword' that will pierce her soul (a huge sorrow, a piercing: you will be torn apart), we should not simply refer it to the fact of seeing her son suffer and die at a young age. It is something more specific, connected with the rest of the prophecy, almost driving in the 'sword'. In fact, we need to bear in mind that while the NRSV translation of the Bible has the words 'a sword will pierce your own soul' at the end, in other translations we can find it at the centre: 'Behold, this child is destined for the fall and rising of many in Israel and for a sign that will be spoken against (yes, a sword will pierce through your own soul also). That the thoughts of many hearts will be revealed' (*New King James Version*).

In the former instance the words are put as a conclusion in a certain sense, not situated within the prophecy of Jesus who will be contradicted. However, if we take account of the difference just indicated, the 'sword' that will pierce Mary's heart means her intimate part in Jesus who will be contradicted and rejected, seeing him amidst ambiguities, and feeling herself torn apart by the Messiah's suffering.

Mary will directly share in Jesus' suffering, then, and be involved in his anguished existence: she will see him opposed by so many people who seemed good and welcoming at the beginning, like the shepherds, and will suffer at the fact that as Messiah, he will be rejected by the leaders of the people.

We glimpse his Mother's life strictly united with the mystery of Jesus and his sufferings, and at the same time from the outside, because she is unable to remedy the situation. She can only passively contemplate her Son's mystery, destined as she is to letting him emerge as a sign of contradiction, without succeeding in bringing him direct assistance.

3) This appears more clearly in the episode involving the twelve-year-old Jesus in the temple. I want to comment particularly on the words: 'Look, your father and I have been searching for you in great anxiety' (2:48).

In reality it is not a case of simple anguish or anxiety: it is much more. It is a word that expresses the painful suffering of the rich man in hell: 'I am in agony in these flames' (Lk 16:24).

Paul uses the same words in his letter to the Romans: 'I have great sorrow and increasing anguish in my heart' (Rom 9:2).

What, then, is Mary's sorrow over the three days she was looking for Jesus? It is a series of sufferings: the mother who has lost her son; the suffering of someone entrusted with responsibility for Jesus and who feels she is lacking something; again, the natural possessiveness of a mother faced with huge disappointment; the son she thought was hers, whom she kept so close, has gone missing without so much as an apology or recognising the grief he is causing.

It is a very painful moment for Mary who understands how complete abandonment to God's word has brought her to an unforeseen situation with regard to Jesus, one almost of misunderstanding, distancing, where her Son speaks to her in language that for her is incomprehensible.

We can also reflect on Mary's feelings when her Son is driven out of Nazareth and humiliated before the whole city (cf. Lk 4:28). She sees Jesus' failure, experiences the suffering of being unable to do anything for him and understands that she is called to passively accept such suffering as a manifestation of the messianic power of Jesus' love: that is, she is preparing herself for the cross.

4) But the hardest blow for Mary, the biggest trial before the cross, we read of in Luke 8:19. It also came from Jesus. Luke is very delicate in describing the episode, by contrast with Mark, and simply explains that his mother and brothers could not reach him because the crowd was too many; so they sent word to him that they were outside and wanted to speak with him. Jesus refused to see them: 'My mother and brothers are those who hear the word of God and do it.'

We cannot deny that these are harsh, hard, severe words.

Yet Jesus does have a heart; in the preceding chapter, for example, he is moved at the death of the only son of a mother from Nain (Lk 7:12). Perhaps he subjected his mother to a severe refusal because of the brothers he wanted nothing to do with.

There is absolute freedom in Christ, a freedom that also counts where his mother is concerned. Mary understands that she has to leave Jesus to his destiny, that she will not have him back except by abandoning him, will not have him back except by continuing to live her discipleship in obedience. Mary is invited to take the road of discipleship and listening, although having the privilege of being his mother.

Mary beneath the cross. Mary in the Church

1) It is clear that she knew and experienced all this, but Jesus repeats it all for her at the cost of emotional strain. Thus, Mary continues to share in Jesus' public life via her *absence*. There are women who follow him and who are mentioned by Luke at the beginning of Chapter 8; Mary is not one of them. We can easily imagine how she would have lived out her role of passivity and adoration of God's will, steeped in suffering at her Son's growing lack of success. 'He learned obedience through what he suffered' (Heb 5:8).

She had been obedient from the beginning, however she still needed to learn and bitterly so, to let God do as he wanted and let her Son do as he wanted. I believe that this may have been part of Mary's 'sword': seeing her own Son nearing the precipice, in extreme danger, in danger of being torn apart, and at the same time she is being forced out, prevented from intervening.

Differently from Peter, Mary accepts her role and perhaps such acceptance is the reason why Luke, who is so careful and profound in reminding us of the roots of Mary's consent, the roots of the whole work of salvation, does not present us with Mary beneath the cross. She remains silent and Luke is silent on her presence at Calvary; the group of women is there but Mary does not have a role for herself.

2) Instead, Luke clearly sees the role of Mary in the Church: at the culminating moment of the community's foundation, she is there with the apostles. We can have a glimpse of how her journey has unfolded. Mary gave herself to God and to Jesus; she gave Jesus to his mission, freed herself of even the least emotional attachment to her Son.

This is why she receives – as Luke recounts it – the gift not of her Risen Son's life but the gift of the primitive community. Purified in her affections, purified of any possible form of control, she is now ready to receive a multitude of sons and daughters. Luke, who does not speak of the scene of the cross presented by John, gets us to understand that Mary, having been freed of everything, having learned to adore the Son given her by the Father and wrenched from her in his love for all humankind, can now open her arms again and *receive her place in the Church* on behalf of other children.

We think of the extraordinary purification she has been through and how she too, a thousand times more than Peter, had to suffer by seeing her Jesus, no longer hers, in the hands of men, handed over to men, killed by men, out of love for all men and women.

3) I would finally like to reflect on the scene in John 19:25-27, that we can understand better at this point. In his very brief presentation of Mary beneath the cross he gives her presence a definitive and perennial value. It makes explicit what Luke has given us to understand: in accepting

that her Son will die, in depriving herself on behalf of humanity, Mary welcomes others; she receives John and opens her heart to receive the Church's children, to be our Mother.

In John, this episode (as with the Pentecost scene in Luke) signifies Mary's return to her Son; at the moment Jesus is lifted up and glorified on the cross, Mary receives the ultimate, definitive consecration of her 'Yes'.

We can consider how the initial *yes* has brought her so far. What an extraordinary course of inner and unforeseeable events for Mary. She could never have expected the travail of being a mother and being separated from her son, having to abandon him into human hands so that God's love would be manifested in him. She would never have thought that she would have to accept that God's love for human beings would be so great, that her Son would suffer and die in such a way. She learns to understand in her flesh that God's love for humankind is infinite, without limits; she is its opportunity and expression. This is why we venerate her as a model capable of introducing us to the love whose flame she has experienced.

'O Mary, we are powerless and silent before your mystery, faced with the inner, awful events that happened to you. You experienced the power of God's love for us; at your own expense you experienced the extent to which your Son abandoned himself into our hands, slipping away from yours. You experienced our wickedness towards him and shared in his goodness, his defenceless dedication. You experienced the infinite power of his love for us, for all men and women.

———

Through your intercession, obtain the grace for us to experience the power of Christ's love and to accept, as you accepted, becoming co-sharers in his powerful action, while foreseeing the abyss of emotion and suffering this involvement could bring with it.

Obtain the grace for us not to rebel at the detachment and purification your Son brings to us, detachment from ourselves, our works, our hopes, our plans. Thus will God's love be able to freely manifest itself in us and others.

We ask you, Mother of Jesus, for a simple, humble, patient heart abandoned to God, a heart able to spread to others its faithful acceptance of God's plan that transforms the world. Amen.'

THE ACCOUNT
IN JOHN'S GOSPEL

1

THE CROSS AND GLORY

Introduction

In this meditation, I would like to offer an introductory glance at various themes so we can enter into John's mindset and gain what I would call a 'spiritual understanding of the Passion.' I will add the proposal for a possible subdivision of the Johannine account into seven episodes.

In a second meditation, I will spend some time with the third episode of the Passion (18:28–19:16), the one John dedicates more space to, and will deal briefly with the episode of Jesus on the cross after his death (19:1-37).

First of all, then, I intend to note some general aspects of the Johannine account that I will identify through presentation of *three themes*, inviting you to bear in mind that two ordinary principles of the Johannine style also hold true for the Passion narrative: the *interpretation of levels,* and his *solemn style*. Let me explain briefly.

John usually presents a grand unified and contemplative vision where various levels merge with one another. It is as if, for the mystical gaze of the seer, the level that is the earthly present life of Christ (to which the apostle is speaking) and the other level of the future Church's life, are in fact merging and seen as a whole. Such a perspective, then, includes present, past and future. In our case, therefore, it includes cross and glory, the cross in the humble life of the Christian, and with the Christian's glorification. The Johannine Passion needs to be meditated upon by drawing attention to this intense merging of levels.

It is undeniable, then, that the Passion account is influenced by a solemn, majestic, at times slow style that is typically Johannine. The facts, while maintaining all their cruelty – the injustice of the suffering Jesus' conviction, the blows he was unjustly dealt, the scourging, the crucifixion – are transfigured in the light of the profound reality they contain. One could almost accuse John of a lack of feeling, of indulging in word play. Nor is there a lack of Johannine irony that becomes even more acute due to the sometimes dramatic, sometimes awkward contrasts that explode within some situations.

Let us not forget, however, that the Synoptics themselves sometimes seem to us to be somewhat pitiless in their representation of the Passion: if we think well about it, there is no heartfelt exclamation or question from them given the sheer dramatic nature of the events. On the other hand, we should recall that the account, when it was put together, had already been absorbed over a lengthy period and lovingly meditated upon. This had meant that the pain of it had been transfigured in contemplation and the New Testament authors are presenting us with a reflection on these mysteries that is already well advanced.

For his part, John seems to insist on the terms of his contemplation of the Christological mystery. He sees the revelation of 'God for us' in the Passion, the completion of the Incarnation: God gave himself to us in his Son to that extent. We come, then, to the themes by means of which John develops his contemplation of the Christological mystery in the Passion.

The theme of glory

We need to call attention above all to the theme of *glory* that we find right from the beginning of the Gospel: 'We have seen his glory' (1:14).

At Cana, too, there was an early manifestation of glory (2:11) that allowed us to see the kind of dimension it would then be manifested within, a context of humility and service, but very different in its dramatic nature. After Cana, all the expectation of the glory that must be revealed is already tending toward the Passion: this will be truly the glorious moment *par excellence.*

Thus, we arrive at the prelude to the Passion (cf. 12:23-28). We can read some lines in the passage that are essential for our understanding of the events. The context is notable: some Greeks want to see Jesus. Jesus replies: 'The hour has come for the Son of Man to be glorified. Very truly, I tell you, unless a grain of wheat falls into the earth and dies, it remains just a single grain; but if it dies it bears much fruit. Those who love their life lose it, and those who hate their life in this world will keep it for eternal life. Whoever serves me must follow me and where I am, there will my servant be also' (12:23-26).

The theme of glory resumes at v. 28: 'Father, glorify your name.' Then a voice came from heaven, 'I have glorified it and I will glorify it again.'

At v. 27, the mystery of Jesus' glory was shown in a context of agitation: 'Now my soul is troubled. And what should I say – Father, save me from the hour?' Then in v. 28: 'Father, glorify your name.'

This glory is about to be manifested in the Passion of Jesus. We note a coming together of paradoxes: the term 'glory' ordinarily means honour, homage, favours, success. The glory of Jesus as described to us, though, passes through infamy, insults, blows and being destroyed at the hands of human beings. It is a paradox that presumes acceptance of the paradoxical nature of the mystery of God among us that is now revealed in its culminating and strongest moments. It is a paradox that can perhaps have light shed on it if we consider two appeals: one of Jesus ('Father, glorify your name') and one at the beginning of the Our Father 'Hallowed be your name'). Supplications of the kind take all their significance from similar ones in the Old Testament: 'Sanctify your name, O God; glorify it' meant: 'Show how powerful you are, God; show that you can save us; show your overwhelming power in your people's difficulties and suffering.'

So, 'Glorify your Son' (17:1) or 'The hour has come for the Son of Man to be glorified' (12:23), given the Old Testament sense, are expressions that could translate as

'Show that your Son is powerful and able to save.'

Now, this glory of God, this great power of the Son, is being manifested in the cross.

Why? John gives us to understand: 'For God so loved the world that he gave his only Son' (3:16), and shows his glory by loving the world, and loving it by giving his Son through the cross. God is revealed in his glorious fullness of love through the total gift Jesus freely makes of himself for us.

The theme of exaltation

A second theme, connected with the preceding one, is that of the cross as *exaltation*, lifting up. I quote three fundamental passages.

1) 'And just as Moses lifted up the serpent in the wilderness, so must the Son of God be lifted up, that whoever believes in him may have eternal life' (3:14).

Note that it is the same purpose for which John wrote his Gospel: 'that through believing, you may have life in his name' (20:31); the purpose is connected with the lifting up of Jesus. Here it has a mysterious and enigmatic character. So, what is this lifting up?

2) In 8:28 this mystery is emphasised once more: 'When you have lifted up the Son of Man, then you will realise that I am he, and that I do nothing on my own.'

The lifting up will mark the moment when it will be truly known who this Son of Man is, whose way of being will copy that of Yahweh, in all and for all ('I am who am' or 'I am he.')

---

3) A further clarification is given during Chapter 12, that is a prelude to the Passion: 'And I, when I am lifted up from the earth, will draw all people to myself' (12:32).

The enigma becomes clear: it is a lifting up on the cross. On the other hand, a new paradox appears: the term 'lifting up' or 'elevation' can also be translated as 'exaltation': in this case it serves to express the elevation to the kingly throne. Jesus' elevation on the cross, then, is a royal exaltation. But while the king elevated to the throne, lifted up on the throne, rules by imposing himself, Jesus rules by attracting. We are faced with a play of ideas that could be frightening because of their dramatic nature but that in reality allow us to see how John has long contemplated the cosmic significance of the mystery of the cross as the centre of attraction in history, the revelation of the meaning of human existence and of the existence of God himself.

The theme of 'the hour'

The third theme – also strictly connected with the preceding ones – is the theme of 'the hour' that already appears in the Cana episode: 'My hour has not yet come' (2:4).

The mystery of the hour of Jesus' glory, however, is present throughout the Gospel; it is enough to think of texts like: 'the hour has come for the Son of Man to be glorified' (12:23), 'The hour is coming' (16:32).

What does this 'hour' represent in Jesus' life? The theme is very rich and complex. There are also exegetical elements to it that are not entirely clear. I would simply say: the 'hour' that accompanies Jesus from the beginning to the end (desire for the hour, the hour about to come, that is announced, that came) expresses the willingness to give his life. From the beginning he is ready to give himself and leans towards the moment of gift that will be his 'hour', that is, the moment foreseen by the Father. Throughout his whole existence Jesus reveals himself as the Son abandoned to the Father, aimed at corresponding totally to the loving plan that he is to manifest to us. When this loving plan asks Jesus for the gift of his life in obedience to the Father, on the cross, his 'hour' will have struck.

The account

I have given you some indications that can introduce us to a meditative reading of the Passion. In any case, since the account is fairly long (two entire chapters) and we are often lost amid the many things we find there, it can be useful as an aid to reading, to keep in mind a possible subdivision of the text into seven episodes. I will offer some paths to follow for each of these which will serve to highlight the aspect John is chiefly insisting on.

1) The first episode (18:1-12) is *Jesus' arrest* (John does not recount the agony in the Garden since he leaves aside the themes of immediate suffering, spending more time on the theme of Christ as revealer). I note three aspects of Jesus' arrest in particular:

a) A paradox: the one they are looking for in order to put him to death offers himself spontaneously. The men look for him, thinking he is escaping, and he goes and gives himself up.

b) Jesus reveals himself as the one who goes to the Passion aware of his divinity: 'I am he' (*egó eimi*). Today exegetes commonly maintain that these words contain a clear allusion to the identity of Yahweh, whose name is, precisely, 'I am who am.' John presents us with Jesus who goes to the Passion gloriously, in the full awareness that he is God; by assuming his divine identity, then, he reveals the mystery of the Father to us.

c) Jesus is concerned with saving his disciples: he is the Good Shepherd who defends his own and does not want them to suffer as he suffers.

2) The second episode (18:13-27) is the result of the intersection of two motifs: *Jesus before the high priests* Annas and Caiphas, and *Peter who denies him*. These motifs alternate through four scenes: Jesus is convicted by the high priests; the scene is interrupted and speaks of Peter; Jesus is questioned by the high priest; again, it speaks of Peter.

We are struck on the one hand by Jesus' courage and on the other by Peter's fear. Jesus shows himself to be a courageous, calm witness; Peter is afraid and denies him. Jesus relies on the Father and therefore appears strong in his attitude of courage, calm and self-giving; Peter relies on himself, and collapses due to his own fragility.

There is also a sorrowful aspect, of its nature more intimate, that John wants to stress. Jesus is relying on his friends: 'Ask those who heard what I said to them; they know what I said.' His disciples, however, step back: 'We do not know who he is.' So there is a clear contrast between the trust Jesus has placed in them and their not deserving such trust.

3) The following episode, the third, is the longest (18:28-19:16): *Jesus before Pilate*, which we will return to in the next meditation. I can anticipate it now, though, by saying that the central theme seems to me to be this: the one who is judged will reign, i.e. he will judge. Human beings are persisting in judging Jesus, and he, even while allowing himself to be judged, is in fact showing that he is their judge and king.

4) The following episode (19:17-22): *the crucifixion*. John insists on the title of the cross to which he dedicates a good number of verses. To me the theme seems to consist of the royal exaltation of Jesus or, if you like, in the contrast between human beings setting out to kill him and the sovereignty he displays.

5) The fifth episode (19:23-30) is the *fulfilment*: at the moment of Jesus' death the realities of salvation are fulfilled. The scene is extremely important. The Scripture is fulfilled: the soldiers divide up his clothes (this is one of the few biblical quotations John insists on). Jesus' Mother is also given to his disciples. With this gift of his Mother to John, the Church has its beginning; a few of Jesus' friends make up the nucleus of the Church he has saved. He can now utter his final words: 'It is finished.'

Then Jesus gave up his spirit. Here is a further ambiguity because Jesus is surrendering his Spirit in the sense of dying, but the expression used by the Evangelist also means: 'Jesus gives the Spirit' in the sense that by his death he is opening the gates to a pouring out of the Spirit. It is the glory of God that is being manifested, since through the death of the Lord the Spirit invades the world.

6) Finally, after death, the ultimate mystery (19:31-37). We note two biblical quotations (John provides these only at extremely important moments), corresponding to the two themes of *water and blood* and the *Lamb of God*. The paschal sacrifice of the true lamb is complete; the new temple from which the water of life flows is now consecrated for humanity.

7) The final episode (19:38-42) closes the account with the Johannine theme of the *courage of friends*. Beginning with Jesus' death, courage is mysteriously revealed in the hearts of those who are his friends. They begin to honour him, even if they were not very consistent during the Passion. Jesus' glory in human hearts, that began beneath the cross with his most intimate friends, spreads to others who take courage and step forward to ask if they can take his body away. 'A mixture of myrrh and aloes weighing about a hundred pounds' represents a disproportionate quantity that serves to show the degree to which Jesus is mourned and venerated by his friends following his acceptance of his painful destiny.

2

JESUS BEFORE PILATE AND THE PIERCING ON THE CROSS

Two characteristic moments of the account according to John are the central episode of the Passion, *Jesus before Pilate*, and the episode of the *piercing by the spear.*

Jesus and Pilate: John 18:28–19:16

Questions

The passage is very long and complex; indeed, the reader cannot escape the thought that John is saying too much. Almost thirty verses to narrate some undoubtedly fundamental facts (Jesus condemned to death), but ones Mark recounts in almost half the space.

The Jews go to Pilate to have Jesus condemned. Pilate questions him and fails to convince himself that he is guilty. He tries to have him freed by acclamation but Barabbas is preferred. Pilate has Jesus scourged. The soldiers mock him as a pretend king. Finally, Jesus leaves the Praetorium and goes to Calvary. These are the facts.

167

What does John want to say by narrating them in such an extended and lengthy manner?

Exegetes are not in agreement with their responses. Some have sought to see in the scene John's intention to describe the psychological drama of human indecision: when faced with the truth Pilate does not listen, is unconvinced, and in the end is overtaken by events. At the centre of the drama, then, is Pilate or in other words the human being: darkness faced with light.

Others prefer to see John's insistence on a theological and political kind of drama with its centre at 19:11: 'You would have no power over me unless it had been given you from above.'

The expression 'from above' is interpreted as alluding to Roman authority. In this case, the theme would coincide with the one that will be developed in the Apocalypse: the opposition between Empire and Church. But really, all the interpretations seem to be imposing later interests on the text.

We need to begin, rather, with an objective reading to see what John's insistences really are, that is, the specific Johannine message when he is describing the most dramatic moment in Jesus' life.

We have said that John gives the impression of a certain wordiness. Some exegetes from last century, when the passage had not yet been analysed in depth, already noted a frequent and even casual mention of Pilate, who often comes and goes from the Praetorium: this coming and going almost provides the narrative with its rhythm.

I point to John 8 vv. 29, 33, 38 and John 19, vv. 1, 4, 9, 13 that all speak of Pilate's movements:

18:29 Pilate exits the Pretorium to meet the Jews;

v. 33: He comes back in and speaks with Jesus (here we have the questions on the kingdom and truth);

v. 38: He goes out again to debate with the Jews about Barabbas;

19:1 Pilate has Jesus scourged (we presume he comes back in: it is the only time there is no explicit mention);

v. 4: He goes out and presents Jesus, saying: 'Look, I am bringing him out to you';

v. 9: He comes back in to question Jesus once more.

Naturally, there is an historical reason that explains these movements of Pilate: the Jews could not enter a Gentile house without contracting a legal impurity that would have prevented them from taking part in the sacred rites about to begin that evening. So, wanting to avoid any contamination they remain outside the palace. Instead Jesus, as an accused man, is not subject to such a scruple and is led inside to the room where audiences are held. However, the audience is partly inside and partly outside. Pilate enters and exits out of respect for the Jews who brought Jesus to him.

However, given this historically based observation, it seems to us that we can note a theological and stylistic elaboration that derives from the Evangelist's specific intention of distinguishing one scene from another. There are at least two reasons suggesting this.

The first emerges from the observation by which, given this way of telling the story 'in blocks', certain events of the Passion, although very serious such as the scourging, are put somewhat in the shade or mentioned in passing, and are only briefly mentioned in the context of the various scenes. Instead, what dominates on the one hand is the figure of Jesus alone and almost silent in the auditorium, and on the other hand the people shouting, while Pilate is in the middle.

The second reason for understanding things this way could be deduced from the fact that mentions of Pilate coming in and out take place at regular intervals, stressing a rhythm (we have already noted this). Now, if we follow the process of these actions to the end, according to this rhythm, we see that we are dealing with *seven distinct scenes*. So, the entire episode presents an orderly, ascending development that culminates in the seventh scene when Pilate says, 'Here is your king' (19:14).

Leaving aside serious themes – like the barely mentioned scourging – the whole episode points to illustrating and celebrating Jesus' kingship.

Also, if the seven scenes are arranged in the order indicated in John's presentation we can easily note a chiastic type correspondence regarding the content, between the first and seventh, second and sixth, third and fifth, while the fourth remains at the centre. I want to say that not only is the final scene (Jesus is king) highlighted, but also the fourth scene (the crowning with thorns) has a particular value: as a farcical royal coronation. So, the text has a partly ascending, partly concentric structure that could seem excessively over the top for our taste. The fact is, however, that we find here the result of a meditation that takes all the events and compares them, arriving at a verbal expression that links them, following the rhythm of the words themselves with a view to helping the contemplation and reconsideration.

We have said that the scenes correspond in the introductory words, the same for each pair of scenes (the first and seventh, second and sixth, etc). They also correspond in terms of their location: the first and seventh take place outside, before the people; the second and sixth in the palace; and the third and fifth before the people once more. Then they correspond in content: the first and seventh are scenes of negation of Jesus where his death is requested; the second and sixth are scenes where Jesus speaks of the kingdom and royal power so the central question further emerges: *how* is Jesus king? *What* is Jesus' *true sovereignty*? The third and fifth scenes contain two declarations by Pilate about Jesus' innocence. The whole process, then, focuses around Jesus. The complexity of the form serves to encourage a deeper understanding of what lies behind the facts of the story so we can grasp their significance.

It is clear, then, that while it is the seventh scene that stands out in the stepwise construction ('Here is your king'), in the concentric structure the scene that stands out is Jesus' 'coronation'. These are the two moments of sovereignty submitted for the attention of someone contemplating the scenes.

So, we begin to understand how this theme of sovereignty is something John has very much at heart. Therefore, the fundamental thematic question is as follows: What is Christ's true sovereignty if he fled the idea when they wanted to make him king, while now he is insistently proclaimed king by the facts and situations? In other words: where is Christ truly the Messiah? Where does the fullness of the messianic triumph come into play? Where is the glory of God in the messianic triumph of the king manifested?

Clearly the most immediate answer that comes to mind is in the resurrection. Nevertheless, John wants us to go beyond this first response and shows us that the Christ truly reigns already in the Passion and as a consequence, the Paschal Mystery is already in operation.

The true sovereignty of Jesus

We can see, then, how the theme of *Christ's true sovereignty* is explored and understood in its progress through the various scenes.

In the second scene it is Jesus who is proclaimed king before Pilate, but one of a special sovereignty not as yet specified. The theme is presented as real but at the same time mysterious.

In the fourth scene, a central one compared with the others, Jesus is crowned with thorns, cloaked in purple and greeted as king. Here the historian reads shame, ignominy and mockery. John instead contemplates the scene as a transfigured one, seeing its transcendent significance; Jesus is shown as king and the soldiers, just when they think they are vilifying him, are fulfilling the plan of salvation. In this ignominious circumstance of Jesus' kingship, it is the love of God that is manifested in our midst, God's glory.

In the following scene, the fifth, Jesus is presented with royal insignia. But Pilate does not yet say: 'Here is your king', as he will say at the end, but 'Here is the man.' What sort of progression does Pilate's declaration denote? Probably on the historical level, a certain sense of compassion shows through these words: 'Here is this poor man, the man people are so afraid of.' Or perhaps, according to others, given that Pilate is not a man accustomed to compassion, there is a sense of contempt for the Jews in them: 'Here is the man you want to get rid of as dangerous, a rebel.'

Nevertheless, on the theological level where John is always filtering the facts through meditation, it is clear that the words have deeper meaning. In fact, Jesus is not called 'man' in the same way as when he was presented to Pilate the first time. Pilate goes out then and says: 'What accusation do you bring against *this man*?' (18:29), but this time he is called *ho ánthropos*: 'here is *the man.*'

This is said of the man there before him, the man wearing the crown, purple, and in the same passage he is called the man who 'has claimed to be the Son of God.' So probably – still staying with John's style – there is an allusion to the title 'Son of Man': here is the man foretold, the man who must come, the one who, with this title as 'Son of Man' evokes the Messiah's juridical and regal power.

In other words, John contemplates in Christ's humiliation the sign of the mysterious power of the Son of Man here on earth. He sees in this contemplation, the *coincidence of opposites* that is the sign of divine works. God has promised this mysterious 'Son of Man', judge and king. Now, within a circumstance of ignominy, he exercises his power of judgement on humanity.

Finally, the last scene, the seventh, that begins with v. 13, is presented with particular solemnity.

Above all, John wants to draw attention to the place where it all happens: we are outside in a place called 'The Stone Pavement' or *gábbatha* in Hebrew, probably an elevated spot known at the time, but one that catches the gaze and mind of the reader.

Secondly, it is important for John to be specific about the time: toward the sixth hour, the time of preparation for the Pasch, the time when the paschal lamb was slaughtered. At the same time, the great mystery is being fulfilled, completed, its truth seen in the signs that happen in the Temple. All this makes us think that we are before an event of huge significance.

From the historical point of view, it is about Jesus being condemned to die: an act of cowardice and injustice. Pilate sits in court, presents Christ as a mock king then abandons him to be crucified. This is how it appears from a first, obvious reading of the passage.

However, if we reread the verses carefully we note at least two details: (1) There really is no conviction because a specific sentence is not pronounced; (2) There is one line that has given the exegetes much to think about and that, to some of them, seems to be deliberately ambiguous: this is the expression *ekáthisen epì bématos* in v. 13, translated by the Vulgate as 'sedit pro tribunali.' While it is commonly thought the sentence means that Pilate sat down, given the closeness of Jesus' name and the possible attribution of an active meaning to the verb *ekáthisen*, it seems that Pilate 'made Jesus sit' in the sense that he installed him on the throne.

In fact, the Ecumenical Bible translates it as: 'He led Jesus outside and installed him on a judge's seat.' The impression one gets from the scene, then, is that the one who seems to be judged is in reality judging humanity. The episode, which on the historical level concludes with Jesus' conviction, on the interpretative level instead makes the glory of Christ shine forth in the humiliation of his death – given the presence of judicial and regal power that is Christ's as the Son of Man, and which John is contemplating.

We are perhaps on the border between exegesis and exegetic creativity, but for some exegetes it seems to be in line with real Johannine interpretation: John has such a paradoxical perspective (because he knew the mystery of God which is paradoxical by comparison with any human action) that he is led to read the signs of Jesus' fulfilment of his messianic mission, even in the most brutal circumstances of his death. Jesus manifests the Father's love in such an unheard-of way that he becomes, by virtue of this love, king and Messiah, source of salvation for humankind whether they accept or reject him. Here we have the messianic enthronement of Jesus the moment he brings to completion his fundamental mission, a mission that consists in manifesting the Father's love to human beings through the complete giving of himself.

By presenting us with the dramatic clash between light and darkness in his Gospel, John the Evangelist leads us to the culminating moment in which darkness seems to triumph: it is humanity's darkest hour. Yet, already at the moment that humankind tries to crush him, in reality the Christ reigns and triumphs. What happens before Pilate, constitutes a sign in which the historian reads death. The believer, instead, reads the fulfilment of Jesus' true mission, his triumph.

Such a range of paradoxes can help us reflect on the paradox that is Christian life, our life: God reigns for us in apparently paradoxical situations and especially in the most paradoxical of them all, that is death. In it we are called to manifest the glory of God, not through words that do not succeed in expressing it but through the very reality of an event that associates us with the moment in which Christ gave himself for us.

Reflecting, then, on the broader significance that Jesus' kingship can have, we can turn our attention to the Synoptic teaching on the kingdom of God. What does 'kingdom of God' or 'kingdom of the Father' mean? It means that God is at the centre of every reality and that all reality is perfectly ordered beneath his divine dominion. This is the 'kingdom of God' that Jesus came to establish. According to the teaching presented in John, Jesus is given dominion precisely when he carries out the supreme service of love and truth. This is also Jesus' 'attraction'. Jesus does not reign by controlling, by extending his influence through power from on high, but reigns by attracting. By making God's love for derelict humanity resplendent in himself, Jesus is able to draw to himself whoever knows how to read the sign, whoever knows how, through meditation on the cross, to read the certainty of being loved by God in his own poverty and dereliction – a situation completely similar to that of the Son.

The thrust of the spear

I propose to meditate on the passage that immediately follows the account of Jesus' death on the cross (19:31-37). It is all over, Jesus is dead and of itself there would be nothing more to tell. Yet John still wants to tell us something that will help us better understand the meaning.

Jesus is dead; the Scripture has been fulfilled in his death and his work is complete. But what does his death signify? The Evangelist sees the transcendent meaning of what has happened in a simple anatomical detail.

Of itself the historical fact is very simple and sufficiently plausible. The Sabbath day is close at hand; the condemned men cannot remain on the cross. According to the custom of the time their legs should be broken. This has been dramatically documented with the discovery some years ago in a tomb near Jerusalem of the bones of a crucified man: it is the first time in the history of archaeology that the bones of a crucified person have been found, especially the leg bones.

On the basis of this, it has also been possible to reconstruct the position of that crucified individual, who was more or less from the time of Jesus (he was probably one of the large number according to Josephus Flavius, who were crucified around Jerusalem a little before 70 A.D.).

The result of the studies on this archaeological find is truly impressive, because in the bones of the condemned man one can almost read the whole of the cruel torture of the cross; one sees the hole made by the nail and the breaking of the bone carried out at the end. John alludes to a reported fact. They did not break Jesus' legs; he was only given a *coup de grace*, a thrust of a spear in the side. What follows cannot be interpreted from a medical point of view: other than blood, some water comes out. At any rate, John does not want to insist on the 'why' of the deed – whether it is miraculous or not; by taking it as reportage he looks for its meaning in the Scriptures.

He asks himself, then, what the significance is of the details that occurred after Jesus' death. 'And you shall not break any of its bones' (cf. Ex 12:46). John is thinking of the paschal lamb. It leads us to contemplate in Jesus' cross the true sacrifice of Israel that perfectly fulfils all the expectations of the Temple. The Temple that is to be destroyed and rebuilt is Jesus himself in whom the sacrifice of the true lamb is accomplished.

More mysterious is the other prophecy: 'they will look on the one they have pierced' (Zech 12:10).

Historically, this is applied to the soldiers and those standing around looking on, and perhaps also to the disciple who as a witness, looked on with a certain curiosity as the crucified Jesus' life gave out. John's thinking, seen through the words of the prophecy, is addressed to all humankind who will look at the crucifix as the full manifestation of God-for-us, of Jesus Christ who is for us to the farthest limit of his love.

The same mystery of blood and water, although not commented on by John with biblical texts, is expressly highlighted: 'He who saw this has testified so that you also believe. His testimony is true and he knows that he tells the truth.'

It certainly has a meaning, but what? Exegetes offer some. John has such a wealth of indications that he never has just one thing in mind: there can be two or even three at the same time, all validly applicable. Water is life; it is the gift of the Spirit; it is, in the baptismal interpretation from Chapter 3 onwards, the sacrament of Baptism. The blood shed in death is the blood of which Jesus said: 'Those who eat my flesh and drink my blood will have eternal life' (6:54).

From the scene John presents us with, then, a first meaning emerges: sacramental life, Baptism and Eucharist, emerges from the death of Jesus. The Church recognises that it receives these gifts from the crucified Lord. The scene probably also has a further significance that Ezekiel's prophecy directs us to: how, according to the promise (Ez 47:1-12), rivers of living water would flow from the Temple – and Jesus picks up precisely these words in v. 7 – so the new water of the Spirit and Life flows from the new Temple destroyed and soon to be rebuilt. In Jesus there is the perfect sacrifice, the perfect Temple, the life of the Church. John has not pushed his meditation explicitly to this point, but what is clearly expressed is the fact that sacramental life flows from Jesus and that the Church is born from it.

We conclude our meditation by asking Jesus to help us grasp the mystery of the spear thrust. Humanly speaking it would seem to be saying: not even in death is Jesus spared, because an implacable and malignant fate is imminent; in fact, this piercing shows the power of the One who sent him on earth and the very power of Jesus who gives life to humanity through the final humiliation inflicted on him.

They are paradoxical and difficult mysteries; only our adoration can, in some way, grasp hold of what the Johannine pointers inspire in us, so rethink the cosmic significance, valid for all of history, of the unique sacrifice of Jesus on the cross.

CONCLUSION

1

THE MESSAGE OF THE RISEN LORD

Jesus' apparitions

If we consider the three readings that have been proclaimed on this most solemn Easter Sunday (Acts 1:1-8; 1 Cor 15:3-10; Jn 20:11-18), we note how Jesus' encounters with different people at different times have been retold.

Jesus appeared to his apostles 'during forty days and speaking about the kingdom of God,' Luke tells us in Acts. And Paul writes that Jesus 'appeared to Cephas and then to the twelve. Then he appeared to more than five hundred brothers and sisters at one time, then he appeared to James,' and then to Paul himself. John the Evangelist recounts Jesus' apparition to Mary Magdalene.

The Risen Lord, then, appears while re-establishing a series of relationships: with individuals, with groups, with the crowd, in order to give everyone the strength and power of the resurrection – the central point of history. Jesus reached this point in his glorious unity with the Father, to then spread it around him.

We, too, are among the people Jesus encounters, because each of us is encountered as an individual, and as a group in the context of the church community.

The Risen Lord calls us by name

Among the many encounters of the Risen Lord, John describes one at length: the one with Mary Magdalene, the first encounter, where Mary represents each of us searching for Jesus Risen, the Lord. It is a search for a complete and definitive meaning of life, for friendship that does not end, for the fullness of God who alone is able to fill our hearts.

And each of us, like Mary Magdalene, if we are caught up in the anxiety of such a search, ends up grieving, frantically looking for signs of hope, signs of God's presence. And the more we seem to be disappointed with the signs, the more we seem to encounter only silence from the other side, the more anxious the search becomes.

Nevertheless, the Gospel shows us how Mary Magdalene's search is mistaken, since she is not making room for God's radical novelty – victory over death. She is looking for Jesus in the tomb, that is, in the context of worldly things, the daily experience she is accustomed to. She is not allowing God to come to her from outside such experience, beyond and above it, inserting himself within it in a fully natural way, but with a force that overcomes all daily experiences.

The Risen Jesus shows himself to Mary in a discreet presence that is an appeal to freedom: he *calls her by name*

– 'Mary!' This way she can feel herself inwardly appealed to. Mary had not recognised him with her eyes but she recognises his voice, because the voice better expresses this inner address.

So, it is through such inner address that we can hear and discover today how God loves us; it is within us that we can hear ourselves called and restored to our deep identity, our vocation as sons and daughters. When the voice of the Risen Jesus strikes us, then our eyes are also opened and we can say with Mary Magdalene:

'I have seen the Lord' and now I know that there is a way for me to follow, a long road of loving Jesus and my brothers and sisters as he loved them.

In this woman's search, therefore, we can see our own search, our efforts, also our sudden joys, our enthusiasm when we feel we can hear Jesus' voice once more within and it agrees with what the voices of the Church, faith, history are telling us.

In these moments of light, joy, inner enlightenment, we understand that Christ's resurrection reveals the meaning of human history to us, of all daily events, reveals to us the direction of all reality, tending towards life, the fullness of expression of our freedom. We understand that in the Risen Jesus a fragment of bodiliness, of history, of the cosmos has been glorified, and that this is the beginning of a new humanity, the destiny of humanity. In fact, it is from Easter that the time for growth of the kingdom begins, the combined work of human freedom and the Spirit of Christ, aiming to embrace the entire universe.

An announcement of great hope

Today, then, in reproposing the Easter proclamation, the Church addresses an *announcement of hope* to the world. Every man, every woman on this earth can see the Risen Lord if they agree to look for him and allow themselves to be sought out. John the Evangelist lets us know that the first creature to discover the signs of the Risen Lord is a woman full of sensitivity, affection, tenderness. Nevertheless, Jesus also reveals himself to groups of people, including five hundred at one time; people, that is, of disparate temperaments, from different walks of life, people in morally diverse situations. The Risen Crucified Lord, only Son of the Father, gives his resurrection to this whole mass of human beings, to brothers and sisters of every time and race. The resurrection, then, marks the passage through which we review our narrow way of perceiving God. We convert from sadness and narrow-mindedness to an extensive vision of the universe opening onto eternity.

In this cry of the resurrection, in our believing in the resurrection, we are invited to change our lives, to change our way of thinking and seeing. We must accept that God's love dissolves fear, that grace forgives sin, that God's initiative comes before any strength of ours and re-animates us, puts us back on our feet after any fall of ours.

This announcement of hope concerns everyone, touches individuals, communities, societies. Today there should no longer be suspicion, sadness, discouragement in us, but the availability to provide room for that incredible and also true hope that comes from Jesus' resurrection, from the message that God is our Father, that he gives life to all his children and that no one is excluded from such an extraordinary gift.

'O Jesus, you who are risen, give to each of us the gift to understand that you are the ultimate, true object of our desires and seeking. Help us to understand what lies behind our problems, what lies within realities that make us suffer.
Help us to understand that it is you we are looking for, the fullness of life; you are true peace whom we are seeking out. We are looking for the person you are, the Son of the Father, so that we too can be trusting, serene sons and daughters. Show yourself to us today in this Eucharist, O Risen Jesus, so that we can hear your voice calling us by name, so that we can allow ourselves to be drawn by you and thus enter into the Trinitarian life where you are with the Father as the only Son, in fullness of the Spirit.'

My wish for you is that the fruit of this Easter may be the fullness of joy and trust in the Risen Christ who makes us children of the Father and opens us to the renewing power of the Holy Spirit.

CARLO MARIA MARTINI
Foundation

The Carlo Maria Martini Foundation came into existence through the initiative of the Italian Province of the Jesuits and with the involvement of the Archdiocese of Milan.

It aims at remembering Cardinal Carlo Maria Martini by promoting knowledge and study of his life and works and keeping alive the spirit that animated his commitment, encouraging experience and knowledge of the Word of God in the context of our contemporary culture.

With this in mind, the Foundation's role is spelt out in a number of specific actions:

- Bringing the Cardinal's works, writings and addresses together in an archive and promoting their study as well as encouraging and authorising their publication.
- Supporting and nurturing ecumenical and inter-religious dialogue, with civil society and non-believers as well, working closely together to understand the indissoluble connection between faith, justice and culture.
- Fostering the study of Scripture involving other disciplines, including spirituality and social sciences.
- Contributing to pastoral and formative projects valuing Ignatian pedagogy and addressed especially to the young.
- Supporting study of the meaning and extended practice of the Spiritual Exercises.

Those who wish to can contribute to the collection of materials (written, audio, video) on Cardinal Martini by indicating initiatives regarding him by writing to segretaria@fondazionecarlomariamartini.it

To subscribe to the newsletter (in Italian) and support the Foundation's activities: www.fondazionecarlomariamartini.it

BIBLICAL MEDITATIONS

A selection of sermons, retreats and meditation texts drawn from the vast work of Cardinal Martini. There is a roundup of biblical personalities from Old and New Testaments, explanations, some chosen topics to accompany reflections on the human being in search of God. The inestimable legacy of a man of prayer and contemporary spirituality.

1. **The Accounts of the Passion.** Meditations
2. **Paul.** In the midst of his ministry
3. **Our Father.** Do not heap up empty phrases
4. **The Apostles.** Men of peace and reconciliation
5. **Abraham.** Our father in faith
6. **Jesus.** Why he spoke in parables?
7. **Elijah.** The living God
8. **Stephen.** Servant and witness
9. **Peter.** Confessions
10. **Jacob.** A man's dream
11. **Jeremiah.** A prophetic voice in the city
12. **Israel.** A people on the move
13. **Samuel.** Religious and civil prophet
14. **Timothy.** Timothy's way

CPSIA information can be obtained
at www.ICGtesting.com
Printed in the USA
BVHW032055080620
581139BV00002B/5/J